PUBLIC LIBRARY
STONEHAM, MASS.
02180/

SPACE EXPLORATION
PROJECTS FOR YOUNG SCIENTISTS

GREGORY VOGT

SPACE EXPLORATION PROJECTS FOR YOUNG SCIENTISTS

PROJECTS FOR YOUNG SCIENTISTS
FRANKLIN WATTS
A DIVISION OF GROLIER PUBLISHING
NEW YORK / LONDON / HONG KONG / SYDNEY
DANBURY, CONNECTICUT

Photographs copyright ©: NASA: pp. 10, 23, 28, 30, 63, 81, 84, 87, 92, 105, 110, 115, 133, 135; Ben Klaffke: p. 33; Unicorn Stock Photos: pp. 47 (Russell R. Grundke), 99 (Frank Pennington); Photo Researchers, Inc.: p. 125 (Dr. Fred Espanak/SPL).

SEP - 1999

Library of Congress Cataloging-in-Publication Data

Vogt, Gregory.
Space exploration projects for young scientists / by Gregory Vogt.
p.   cm. — (Projects for young scientists)
Includes bibliographical references and index.
Summary: Suggests projects demonstrating such outer space principles and phenomena as gravity wells, rocket propulsion, and planetary motion.
ISBN 0-531-11233-0
1. Space sciences—Juvenile literature.   2. Outer space—Exploration—Juvenile literature.   3. Astronautics in cosmic physics—Juvenile literature.   (1. Space sciences—Experiments.
2. Experiments.)   I. Title.   II. Series.
QB500.22.V643   1995
520'.78—dc20   95-23328
                                                                  CIP AC

Copyright © 1995 by Gregory Vogt
All rights reserved
Printed in the United States of America
6 5 4 3 2 1

CONTENTS

———————

WITH RESPECT AND GRATITUDE,
I DEDICATE THIS BOOK TO THE MEN AND WOMEN
OF THE NASA AEROSPACE EDUCATION SERVICES
PROGRAM. THEY HAVE MADE THE WORLD A BETTER
PLACE BY INSPIRING MILLIONS OF YOUNGSTERS
TO DREAM AND BY PREPARING THEM FOR THEIR
DESTINY IN SPACE.

———————

1

THE RIDE
OF YOUR LIFE

It's T minus 31 seconds. You are strapped into your seat in a reclining position on the space shuttle orbiter. But you have little time to think about the adventure you are about to begin. Running through your mind are all the procedures for evacuating in the event of an emergency. Control of the final countdown shifts from the launch control center to the onboard computers. Critical engine checks are being made automatically at a furious rate.

At T minus 6.6 seconds, the main engine ignition sequence begins. Engines 3, 2, and 1 ignite at 120 millisecond intervals. More than 1 million liters of water begins spraying over the launch pad to keep it from catching fire in the impending rocket blast.

Because of the slightly angled thrust of the main engines, you feel your vehicle tilt in the direction of your feet. The vehicle springs back to the vertical position, and the solid rocket boosters ignite. Blasting more than 28 million newtons of thrust, the five engines lift you and the six other astronauts onboard in a giant leap off the launch pad. In seconds, you clear the launch pad tower, and the main engines turn the vehicle in the right direction for orbit.

The space shuttle blasts off.

You are one of three earth scientists on the shuttle's mid-deck, where you can only feel and hear what is happening. Your view to the outside is a circular window through the side hatch. To look out, you have to turn your head sharply to the left. It's not easy to do inside your orange suit and helmet, especially when you are experiencing an acceleration of more than two times Earth's gravity, or 2 g's. The astronauts on the flight deck, however, have an excellent view of scattered clouds flashing by. They see the blue sky turn to bluish gray and then black in only 30 seconds.

At T plus 8 minutes and 30 seconds, the main part of the launch is over. The solid rocket boosters and the external tank have dropped away. In a few minutes, two small orbital maneuvering engines will fire, accelerating you into your final orbit at an altitude of 222 kilometers and an angle of 57 degrees with Earth's equator.

With the g-forces of liftoff now gone, you breathe more easily. Your head, arms, and legs feel incredibly light. A pen you are holding to take notes drifts away. The view from space is more than you could have hoped for. You can see hundreds of thousands of square kilometers of land, water, and clouds at a time. The colors are astoundingly brilliant, and you recognize entire countries that you have seen only from maps before.

That vibrant globe will be your target for the next eight days. You and your fellow crewmates will be operating radar instruments in the orbiter's payload bay to help you and scientists on the ground learn about Earth's environment. The mission will supply a wealth of data on the physical, chemical, and biological processes at work in volcanoes, ocean currents, glaciers, rain forests, deserts, grasslands, and urban areas. And it will fuel scientists' research for several years to come.

AN AGE-OLD DREAM

Fifty years ago, your space voyage wouldn't have been possible. The first unmanned rockets, carrying scientific instruments, weren't able to reach outer space until the 1950s, even though rockets had been invented about 750 years earlier. The first human in space, the Soviet Union's Yuri Gagarin, made his one-orbit voyage on April 12, 1961.

Today, up to seven American astronauts routinely orbit Earth for about two weeks at a time, and Russian cosmonauts spend months onboard the Mir space station. We are well into the space age. It has opened the door to a universe of new scientific discoveries and technological developments.

Getting into space tc conduct research firsthand is a wonderful dream that has already come true for some scientists, and may someday come true for you. So far, only a few hundred people have actually traveled into outer space. Even if you don't get to go into space, you can still conduct space research, as thousands of scientists do every year. They design the research instrumentation carried aboard the space shuttle or analyze the data sent back to Earth by satellites and space probes.

If you are interested in space age research, either for a future career or just for the fun of it, this book is for you. It will give you a small window into the incredibly broad and varied space field, focusing on some of the exciting disciplines involved. What's more, it will help you understand the principles of rocketry and space flight.

But you will not be just reading words and looking at pictures. This is a handbook for taking action. It is filled with projects that will teach you all about space exploration and space science. In most cases, the questions the projects raise can be answered only by doing the projects yourself. They will challenge you to make discoveries and lead you into unexpected directions.

Many of these projects would make excellent entries for science fairs. You will find lots of practical tips and instructions on how to carry them out. In doing the projects, you will get a taste for the exciting world of space-age science.

You will notice that the book in most cases uses metric units and gives no English equivalents. The reason for this is that it is very important to become comfortable with metric units if you want to pursue space research. Although NASA engineers still use English units, astronomers use metric units exclusively. The book gives English units when specifying parts that are available only in English unit sizes.

Use the following table if you want to convert metric to English units.

METRIC-TO-ENGLISH CONVERSION

1.0 meter = 3.28 feet = 1.09 yards

1.0 centimeter = 0.394 inches

1.0 kilometer = 0.62 miles

1.0 kilometer per hour (kmph) = 0.62 mph

1.0 kilopascal = 0.15 pound per square inch

2

PENDULUMS AND PLANETS

By now, you have probably taken at least one course in science. It's likely that your teacher filled the class with experiments and demonstrations that helped you make lots of discoveries about the world.

Your teacher probably spent a little time talking about the scientific method, which is simply the way scientists carry out their investigations. Unfortunately, the discussion of the method can get a little boring. It's somewhat similar to reading the rule book for baseball. The fun comes from doing, not reading.

Here's a simple experiment you can do that will show you the scientific method. The experiment involves making a pendulum. A pendulum is an object that swings freely on one end while the other end is held in place. You've probably seen a pendulum in a grandfather clock; it's the brass disk that swings from side to side.

You might be wondering what pendulums have to do with scientific research, much less space exploration. They have a lot to do with both. Pendulums can teach us about gravity and give clues to why the planets orbit the Sun the way they do.

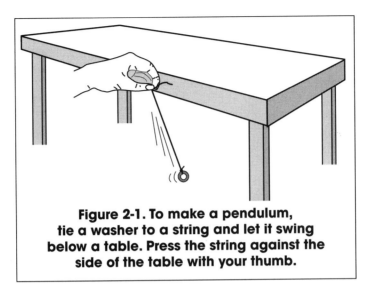

**Figure 2-1. To make a pendulum,
tie a washer to a string and let it swing
below a table. Press the string against the
side of the table with your thumb.**

The Period of a Pendulum

Tie one end of a piece of string to a large washer. Tie a knot at a distance of 30 centimeters (cm) from the center of the washer. Using your thumb, hold the knot against the edge of a table and let the pendulum swing below as in Figure 2-1. Now start thinking like a scientist. Observe what happens. Do you notice any pattern to the swings? How long does it take the pendulum to swing from one side to the other and back again? This time is the pendulum's *period.*

Like you, scientists begin their research by making observations. *Observation* is the first step in the scientific method. *Collecting data,* such as the pendulum's period, is a big part of making observations.

Both observation and data collection are essential to scientific research. For example, an astronomer would not be able to

> *Materials*
>
> - Heavy string
> - Metric ruler
> - 5 large metal washers
> - Stopwatch or watch with second hand
> - Table
> - Scissors

conceive of a black hole in space without first making observations and collecting data on such things as gravity and atoms. In our experiment, observation of a pendulum's period can lead you to find the relationship between period and pendulum length. This, in turn, can provide insights into gravity, as well as the planetary orbits. Let's continue.

The next step in your experiment is to ask *questions*. Let's concentrate on just one question here. Is there a relationship between the mass of the washer and its period? In other words, if the washer were heavier, would the pendulum swing faster? To find out, you must design an experiment. Proper scientific procedure requires that you formulate a *hypothesis* that you can test. A hypothesis is a tentative explanation for the observations you have made so far.

For example, you might propose the hypothesis: *the greater the mass of the pendulum, the faster it will swing; hence, the shorter its period.* This hypothesis is testable. Being able to test your hypothesis is important. If you proposed that the greater the mass of the pendulum, the faster it will swing on Mars, you would not be able to find out whether your hypothesis were true. Since your chances of going to Mars are pretty slim, that hypothesis would be untestable.

Let's test the original hypothesis through an *experiment*. The experiment is simple. Measure the period of the pendulum with one washer attached to it. Then measure the period with two washers; then three, four, and finally five washers. It is very important that you have *controls* on your experiment. Controls are a way of making sure that you are varying only the quantities involved in your hypothesis.

For example, if you were not careful to make the length of the string identical in each pendulum, any change in period you see might be caused by the variation in length. You want to see only the effect of the mass of the pendulum. So make sure you use the same type of string, precisely the same length of string, and identical washers in your experiment. Also, do each test run in the same spot and in still air; the movement of the air around the pendulum could have an effect, too.

Start with the pendulum and one washer. Pull the pendulum a short distance to one side and release it. Determine how many full swings, back and forth, the pendulum completes in 30 seconds (s). Can you guess why 30 s was chosen?

Now without changing the length of the pendulum, attach a second washer to it. Again, measure the number of full swings for 30 s. Be sure to pull the pendulum to the side the exact same distance you did the first time. This is another control in your experiment. Repeat the test with three, four, and five washers. To determine the period of each pendulum, divide 30 by the number of full swings. Plot your results on a graph as period versus the number of washers.

What did you learn from the experiment? Did you confirm or reject the hypothesis that the mass of a pendulum affects its period? Either way, the results of the experiment provided you with new information. That's what the scientific method is really about—gaining reliable information through an organized and controlled process.

PENDULUMS AND GRAVITY

Scientists have studied pendulums for years. One of the first scientists to investigate them was Galileo Galilei. Galileo, an Italian astronomer and physicist who lived about 400 years ago, is better known for being the first to look at the heavens through a telescope and for proving that Earth travels around the Sun. You will soon see that there is a connection between pendulums and the motions of the planets.

One day in church, Galileo's attention was riveted on a chandelier whose candles had just been lighted. The chandelier was gently swinging from side to side. Wondering whether the swings of the pendulum were regular, or periodic, Galileo timed them using his pulse.

He found that the swings did indeed occur at regular intervals, and further scientific investigations led him to the following equation:

$$T = 2\pi \sqrt{\frac{l}{g}}$$

In this equation, T stands for the period of the pendulum. The length of the pendulum is l, and the acceleration of gravity is g. Does this equation agree with the results of your pendulum experiment? Does mass have any role in determining the period of a pendulum? Try solving for T for your pendulum. The value of l was 30 cm. The value of g is 9.8 meters per second squared (9.8 m/s², or 980 cm/s²). Use 3.14 as the value of π, or pi. You will probably need a calculator with a square-root key to work out the problem. As an example, we will calculate T for a pendulum 20 cm long.

$$T = 2(3.14) \sqrt{\frac{20}{980}}$$

$$T = 0.90 \text{ seconds}$$

How does your measured value for T compare with your calculated value?

One of the exciting things about scientific principles is that they apply all over the universe. In other words, this pendulum formula should work anywhere. Even though we can't travel to Mars yet, we can determine what the period of your pendulum would be on Mars. The gravitational pull on Mars is about 0.38 times as strong as the pull on the surface of Earth. Solve for T for a 30-cm pendulum on Mars.

Here's a challenging problem that will impress your teachers if you can solve it. Imagine that you are standing on one of the moons in our solar system. You determine that a 20-cm pendulum has a period of 2.19 s. What is g for that moon? In an astronomy reference book, look up the acceleration of gravity for the various planets in our solar system. What would the period of the 20-cm pendulum be on each planet?

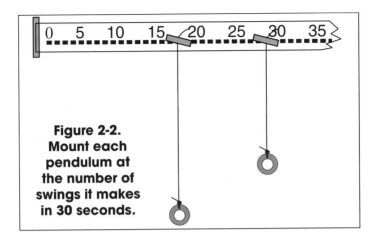

Figure 2-2. Mount each pendulum at the number of swings it makes in 30 seconds.

Pendulums All in a Row

Draw a straight line more than 1 meter long across a long strip of white paper. Place marks on the line at 2-cm intervals. Label the first mark "0," and every fifth mark after that, "5," "10," "15," and so on, until you reach "60." Find a wall on which masking tape won't damage the paint, and tape the paper to it.

Make 15 string-and-washer pendulums, with one washer on each pendulum. Vary the lengths of the pendulums by tying the knot at a distance from the washer center of 5 cm for the first pendulum, 10 cm for the second, 15 cm for the third, and so on. The longest pendulum should be 75 cm long.

Start the experiment with the first pendulum. As in the previous experiment, count the number of full swings it makes in 30 s. Then tape the pendulum to the line on the wall, as shown in Figure 2-2. If the pendulum swung 15 times in 30 s, tape the pendulum at the "15"

Materials

- Several meters of string
- 15 large washers
- Metric ruler
- Scissors
- Stopwatch or watch with second hand
- Table
- White paper
- Marker pen
- Masking tape

mark. Make sure you tape the knot over the horizontal line. Repeat these steps for each pendulum. When you start the pendulum swinging, make sure you always pull it the same distance to the side no matter what its length is.

When all the pendulums have been mounted on the wall, study the pattern they create. You have actually made a graph. What is the relationship between the length of the pendulum and the number of swings? Is your answer supported by Galileo's pendulum formula, which appeared just before this experiment?

Leave your pendulum graph on the wall. You may make an interesting discovery if you compare it to the gravity well you make in the next project.

If you have ever visited a science and technology museum where visitors are encouraged to touch the exhibits, you probably have experimented with a gravity well. It is a large circular dish that curves inward into a steep hole. Usually, the exhibit invites visitors to roll coins into the well. The coins circle around and around the well and finally, about 30 seconds later, drop through the hole into a collection box. It is a fascinating exhibit that can teach you about the motions of planets and satellites.

Making a Gravity Well

To construct your own gravity well, you'll need a large wooden, metal, or plastic bowl that you can drill a hole through. Drill a small hole in the exact center of the bottom of the bowl. Get a piece of heavy string about 20 cm long and tie a knot in one end of it. Slip the other end through a bead that is larger than the hole in the bowl.

Next, cut a large circle out of a heavy, three-ply garbage bag. The circle should be slightly larger than the diameter of the bowl. In the center of the plastic, punch a small hole that the string, but not the bead, can pass through. Coat the edge of the plastic around the small hole with rubber cement and let it dry. Also coat the bottom of the bead with rubber cement to

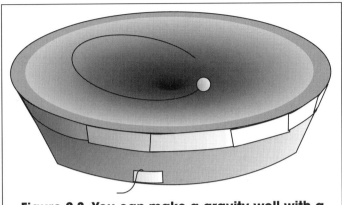

Figure 2-3. You can make a gravity well with a bowl and a plastic garbage bag.

keep it in place next to the knot. Give both the hole and the bead second coats of rubber cement. Then with the plastic inside the bowl, thread the string through the hole in the plastic and through the hole in the bowl. The bead should now rest on the plastic on the inside of the bowl.

With short pieces of masking tape, each about 5 cm long, tape the plastic over the bowl to form a "drum head." Try to align the hole in the plastic directly over the hole in the bowl. As you add more tape, stretch the plastic so that it is drum tight.

Pull on the string hanging outside the bowl to bring the cement on the bead in contact with the cement around the plastic hole. This should bond the bead and plastic together. Now, pull harder on the string and watch what happens to the plastic surface. As shown in Figure 2-3, it

Materials
• 3-ply trash bag
• Large wooden, metal, or plastic bowl
• Masking tape
• Heavy string
• Large bead
• Rubber cement
• Drill and small bit
• Small marbles or ball bearings
• Paper
• Scissors

takes on the shape of a gravity well. Why did it take that shape?

Pull the bead part of the way toward the bottom of the bowl and hold it there by taping the string to the bottom of the bowl. Set the bowl on a level surface and gently roll a small marble across the plastic. Observe what happens to the marble. Try making the marble orbit the bead.

Your gravity well is a model of the solar system. What does the bead represent? What does the marble represent? What does the sloped surface of the plastic represent? Where does the marble roll faster? Slower?

Compare the shape of the gravity well with the shape of the pendulums hanging on the wall. Also, compare it to the graph you drew in the first project on p. 19. Do you see any similarities? Can you guess how pendulums relate to planets orbiting the Sun?

As an interesting follow-up project, make a larger gravity well out of a barrel or large trash can. Thread two or three beads through the plastic to represent a solar system with more than one sun in the center.

The shape of the plastic in the gravity well simulates the gravitational pull the Sun exerts at different distances from it. The curve in the plastic is gentle at the rim but very steep in the middle. Similarly, the gravitational pull is small far away from the Sun, but very large close to the Sun. In other words, the force of gravity is much stronger near the center of the solar system than it is where Pluto hangs out.

When a planet moves closer to the Sun, the increased gravity causes it to move faster. You can see this effect in the gravity well. Near the rim, the marble rolls slowly, but it picks up speed as it rolls toward the middle.

Gravity is a force of attraction between any two entities with mass. The greater the mass of the objects, the greater the gravitational attraction they have for each other. And the closer they are to one another, the greater the attraction. Because the Sun is so massive, its gravitational force holds Earth in orbit at a distance of about 150 million kilometers (km) away, as well as Pluto at a distance of about 5.90 *billion* km.

Standing on Earth, you sense the gravitational attraction of Earth as your weight. Without Earth's gravity, you would have no weight—only mass. When an object falls near the surface of Earth, it accelerates at a constant rate because of Earth's gravity. This acceleration g—approximately 9.8 m/s^2—is commonly referred to as 1 g, meaning one Earth gravity.

On a smaller body, such as Earth's moon, the acceleration due to gravity is less because its mass is considerably less. The gravity on the moon is about one-sixth the magnitude of g on Earth's surface. Check a reference book to find the surface gravity of the other planets in our solar system. What would you weigh if you could stand on each of the planets? Try to relate the gravitational force on each planet to its size and mass.

The gravity well simulates only the Sun's gravity and assumes that all the planets, represented by the marble, have the same mass. But since the Sun is so much more massive than the planets, the model is a good approximation of the forces in the solar system.

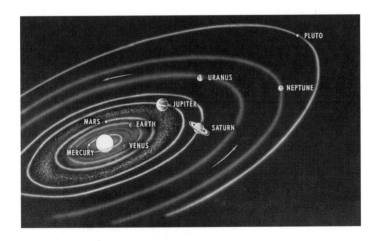

The planets orbit the Sun as shown.

As you practice with the gravity well, you will find it is much easier to create an elliptical orbit than a circular orbit. Even when the orbit appears circular, it is still slightly elliptical in shape. The same holds true for the orbits of planets, moons, and satellites in space. The first person to discover that planets travel in elliptical orbits was a German astronomer named Johannes Kepler, who lived around the turn of the seventeenth century.

The Path of a Planet

An ellipse looks like a slightly squashed circle. To draw an ellipse, stick two sturdy pins into a piece of paper taped to a piece of wood or thick cardboard. The pins should be a short distance from each other as shown in Figure 2-4. Then place a small loop of string around the pins. With your pencil tip inside the loop, draw a shape around the pins, keeping the string taut as you draw.

Examine the shape of the ellipse you just drew. How does it compare to a circle? Try drawing another ellipse with the pins a little farther apart. What shape did you

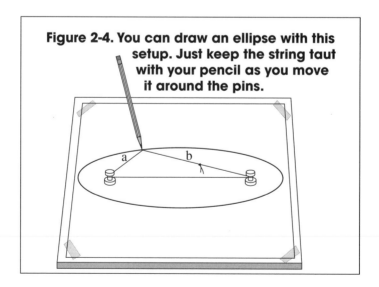

Figure 2-4. You can draw an ellipse with this setup. Just keep the string taut with your pencil as you move it around the pins.

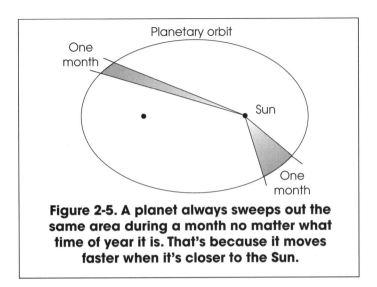

Figure 2-5. A planet always sweeps out the same area during a month no matter what time of year it is. That's because it moves faster when it's closer to the Sun.

get? What would happen if you moved the pins even farther apart? How about if you moved the pins together in the middle?

The shape of the ellipse depends upon the size of the loop and the distance separating the two pins. The two pins represent the *foci* of the ellipse. The foci and the loop size define the ellipse, just as a circle is defined by its center and radius.

Kepler's first law of planetary motion states: *Planets orbit the Sun in the shape of an ellipse with the Sun located at one focus.*

That means the Sun is located at one of the foci of Earth's elliptical orbit. If you could draw an ellipse the size of Earth's orbit, the Sun would be located where one of the pins is.

Kepler discovered two other laws that relate to how fast planets orbit the Sun. Figure 2-5 shows a typical orbit of a planet around the Sun. In the part of its orbit far from the Sun, the planet moves slower than in the part that is closer to the Sun, as the gravity well demonstrated. If you could watch the planet for one month in both near and far parts of the orbit, you would find that it sweeps out the shaded areas shown in the figure. It turns out that these areas are equal to each other. How could you prove that? No matter what month of the year you look at, the area will be the same. This is Kepler's second law of planetary motion: *Planets sweep out equal areas in equal time.*

The important implication of this law is that the velocity of an orbiting planet or an interplanetary spacecraft is affected by its distance from the Sun. If you were designing a space mission to rendezvous with the planet Mercury, for example, you would have to know the velocity and location of the planet at the time you want the spacecraft to arrive. The distance between Mercury and the Sun varies by more than 22 million km in each orbit, so Mercury's velocity changes radically as it swings around the Sun. You want to make sure your spacecraft will be traveling at the correct speed when the rendezvous takes place. Going too fast or too slow will ruin the mission.

Kepler's third law gives the relationship between a planet's distance from the Sun and the time it takes to make one revolution of the Sun. This time is called its orbital period. The third law of planetary motion states: *The square of the orbital period of a planet is directly proportional to its average distance from the Sun cubed,*

or $p^2_{yr} = a^3_{a.u.}$

In this equation, the orbital period, p, is given in years, and a, the planet's average distance from the Sun, is given in astronomical units, or a.u. One a.u. is the average distance from Earth to the Sun. Since Pluto is approximately 39.5 times farther from the Sun than is Earth, Pluto is 39.5 a.u. from the Sun. According to this law, planets farther from the Sun take longer to make their orbits than planets closer to it. Check it out for yourself by looking at a planetary data chart listing distance from the Sun and the time to make a revolution. Compare these values for the various planets.

Can you now see the connection between the period of a pendulum and the period of a planet?

3

ROCKETING INTO SPACE

Although Earth's atmosphere permits reasonably clear views of the planets and stars of our universe, looking outward from Earth is just not the same as actually being in outer space. No Earth view can fully replace the thrill astronauts experience when they set foot on the moon. Nor can it substitute for the scientific data collected by robot spacecraft probing distant worlds. Traveling through outer space is one of humankind's oldest dreams.

Often, early dreams of space travel were fantastic. In old stories and poems, people flew into space by flapping wings, by using "antigravity substances," by riding birds or flying horses, or by being launched with heavy springs. One of the most fantastic space exploration stories ever written is by Jules Verne. He told of a 900-foot-long (274-m) cannon that fired a bullet-shaped space capsule, with three astronauts inside, around the moon and back. Verne's story, like so many others, lacked any basis in reality. In such a situation, the astronauts inside would have been crushed to death by the force of the explosion in the cannon.

When it came time to actually travel in space, most of the fantastic ideas of the past were rejected. Scien-

Apollo 11 astronauts saw this view of Earth shortly before they landed on the moon in 1969.

tists knew there was really only one way to travel through outer space. They had to rely on an ancient invention—rockets.

The first rockets were probably invented by the Chinese. It is believed that in the first century A.D. they had a simple form of gunpowder made from saltpeter, sulfur, and charcoal dust. The Chinese used the fast-burning powder mostly for fireworks in religious and other festive celebrations. They filled bamboo tubes with the mixture and tossed them into fires to create explosions. Some of those tubes probably failed to explode and skittered out of the fires, propelled by the gases and sparks produced by the burning gunpowder.

Perhaps watching these reactions gave the Chinese the idea to experiment with the gunpowder-filled tubes for other purposes. At some point, the tubes were attached to arrows and launched with bows. Soon it was discovered that these gunpowder tubes could launch themselves just by the power of the escaping gas. It was then that the true rocket was born.

ROCKET SCIENCE

A rocket, in its simplest form, is a chamber enclosing a gas under pressure. A small opening at one end of the chamber allows the gas to escape. The escaping gas provides a thrust that propels the rocket in the direction opposite the movement of the gas. You can see this effect by doing the following project.

Balloon Rocket

Balloons are excellent tools for learning the basics of rocket flight. Inflate a balloon, pinch it closed, and then let go of it. What happened? First, you inflated the balloon with air that was compressed by the balloon's rubber walls. While you held the nozzle closed, all forces were balanced. The outward-directed force of the compressed air inside the balloon was balanced by the inward-directed forces of the balloon's rubber walls and outside air pressure as shown in Figure 3-1.

When you released the nozzle, the contracting balloon forced the air out through the opening. The reaction to this force propelled the balloon in the opposite direction. This is precisely what occurs in rocket propulsion.

As the balloon flew off, it followed an erratic path. What can you do to stabilize the balloon so that it will fly in a straight line? Try attaching control devices, such as paper, tape, straws, strings, or any other lightweight materials you can find. Attach them to various spots on the balloon. Keep experimenting until you find a technique

Materials

- Several long balloons
- Cellophane tape
- Paper
- String
- Scissors

that works. On what part of the balloon did you attach your stability devices? Would those devices work if they were attached somewhere else?

The gases escaping from the back of a rocket propel it forward.

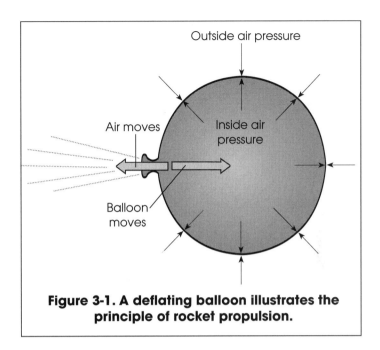

Figure 3-1. A deflating balloon illustrates the principle of rocket propulsion.

The scientific principle behind the propulsion of the balloon and rockets was discovered by the great English scientist Isaac Newton during the latter part of the seventeenth century. He formulated this principle as the third of three laws of physical motion. His first two laws will become important in later chapters. Newton's third law states: *Every action has an equal and opposite reaction.* In the case of the balloon, the force of the air escaping from the rear of the balloon produced an equal force pushing the balloon forward—the direction opposite the motion of the gas.

This principle can be seen in many situations in everyday life. Have you ever stepped off a small boat that was not tied properly to a pier? Your movement toward the pier caused the boat to move away from the pier.

If you have a skateboard, try standing on it while it is not moving, and then leaping forward from it. Your leap is an *action*, as specified in Newton's third law. The skateboard responds to that action by traveling some distance in the opposite direction. This is called a *reaction*. The force of the reaction is equal to the force of the action.

It might appear that the reaction of the skateboard is greater than your action because it travels a greater distance than you do. But the action and reaction that Newton refers to are forces. The acceleration a force produces depends on the object's mass, as you will see in our discussion of Newton's second law. You move a shorter distance than the skateboard because your mass, or weight, is much greater than the skateboard's. Hence, your acceleration is less.

In rockets, the action is the force that expels gas out of the engine. The reaction is the force that propels the rocket in the opposite direction. The pressure building up inside the rocket engine pushes on the gas, and the gas in turn pushes the rocket in the opposite direction. To lift a rocket off the launch pad, the action, or thrust, produced by the engine must be greater than the weight of the rocket. In space, however, even tiny thrusts will cause the rocket to change direction because its effective weight is so small.

One of the most common misconceptions about rockets is that they work by pushing against the air. People often ask how rockets can fly in space where there is no air for them to push against. Anyone who understands the third law knows that air has nothing to do with creating rocket propulsion. In fact, air only hinders it. In the skateboard example, air friction worked against the skateboard motion, slowing it down. Friction of the wheels rolling on the ground also slowed the skateboard. Friction is a force known as *drag* that always works against the direction of motion.

Rockets work better in empty space than in air because in space they don't have to fight drag. The exhaust gases can also escape freely, without having to push against any air. When flying through the atmosphere, some of the rocket's energy must be expended in pushing the surrounding air out of the way.

If you leap forward from a stationary skateboard, the skateboard moves backward. Your action has produced an equal reaction.

Figure 3-2. This drawing shows an operating Hero engine in first-century Greece.

One of the oldest rocket propulsion devices is the Hero engine, invented in the first century by the Greek scientist Hero of Alexandria. Hero's engine rotated as a result of the propulsion produced by escaping jets of steam, as shown in Figure 3-2.

You can make your own Hero engine in the following project.

Hero Engine

Your modern version of the Hero engine will be made out of a copper toilet-tank float. Since many floats are now made of plastic, you may have to go to several hardware or plumbing stores to find a copper one. This project involves metalworking and soldering, so enlist the help of someone who knows these techniques.

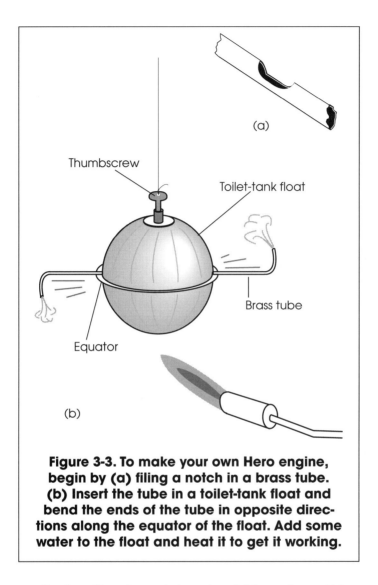

Figure 3-3. To make your own Hero engine, begin by (a) filing a notch in a brass tube. (b) Insert the tube in a toilet-tank float and bend the ends of the tube in opposite directions along the equator of the float. Add some water to the float and heat it to get it working.

Begin with a brass tube about 30 cm long. Using a metal file, file on the midpoint of the brass tube, making a notch that cuts halfway through the tube as in Figure 3-3a. Do not file the tube in half! On the float, drill two small holes slightly larger than the tube diameter.

Place the holes directly opposite each other on the equator of the float. **Caution:** *Make sure you wear safety glasses when drilling.*

Slide the tube through the two holes so that equal lengths protrude out the sides of the float. To fix the tube in place, you will need a propane torch and some solder. Wearing safety glasses and gloves, heat the tube using the torch near the holes in the float. Touch the solder to those areas so that it melts and seals the holes around the tubes. You may need to prepare the metal surfaces with liquid solder flux before applying the solder.

Materials

- Copper toilet tank float (available from hardware stores)
- Thumbscrew, 1/4 inch
- Brass tube, 3/16 ID, 12 in (30.5 cm) (from hobby shops)
- Solder and flux
- Fishing line
- Drill and bit
- Metal file
- Propane torch
- Safety glasses
- Leather gloves

After the solder has cooled, heat the tube about 2 cm from each end. With pliers, carefully bend the tube tips in opposite directions so that they are in line with the equator of the float. Bend the tubes slowly so that they do not crimp.

Take a 1/4-in thumbscrew and drill a small hole through its flat part. Tie a long piece of fishing line to the screw through the hole. Also, drill a 1/4-in (6-mm) hole through the threaded connector at the top of the float. Add a small amount of water to the float through the hole. Then seal the hole by twisting the thumbscrew into the connector. The Hero engine is ready.

Hang the engine by the fishing line. Before heating the engine, test it by blowing through one end of the tube. If air does not come out the other end, the tube is blocked. **Caution:** *Do not use the engine!* Most likely, the blockage is caused by a crimp in the tube; if so, you will have to insert a new tube and start over.

If air flows through the tube, gently heat the bottom of the float with the torch. Watch what happens to the engine after a minute or two of heating when steam begins to emerge. Be careful not to operate the engine too long because it is unbalanced and may wobble out of control. If it begins to wobble, remove the heat.

What do you think would happen if you used a smaller-diameter tube for the engine? What would happen if the tube were larger? Can you think of any modern-day applications for the Hero engine?

The Hero engine operates on the same principle as space rockets. The only significant difference between them is the way the pressurized gas is produced. In rockets, the gas comes from burning solid or liquid propellants. When we think of rockets, we don't usually think of balloons and Hero engines. We think of the giant vehicles that carry satellites into orbit and spacecraft to the moon and planets. You can make a rocket more like those in the following project.

2-Liter-Bottle Rocket

You can create a compressed-air rocket from a 2-liter soft-drink bottle by attaching a tire valve to its plastic cap. If you pump air into the bottle and then release it, it will be propelled through the air as shown in Figure 3-4.

Begin by preparing the tire valve. First, remove the needle valve. It simply unscrews from inside the stem. It may be helpful to use a small knife as a probe to help unscrew the valve. Once removed, the needle valve is no longer needed.

Materials
• 2-liter plastic soft-drink bottle
• Tubeless tire valve stem, 1-1/4 in (3 cm) long (TR no. 413 from auto supply stores)
• Electric drill
• Drill bits (5/32 and 9/16 in)
• Vise
• Bicycle air pump with lever-type valve and air pressure gauge (not bicycle frame pump)
• Safety glasses

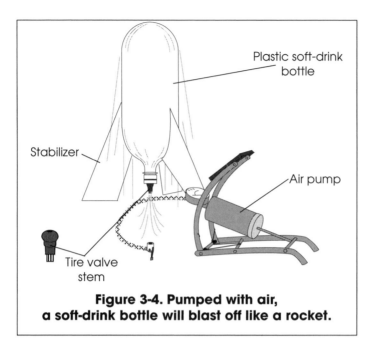

**Figure 3-4. Pumped with air,
a soft-drink bottle will blast off like a rocket.**

While holding the valve stem in a vise, carefully enlarge the hole through the center of the brass part of the stem using an electric drill and a 5/32-in bit. Wear safety glasses when drilling out the stem.

Next, drill a 9/16-in hole through the center of the plastic cap from the bottle. Push the valve stem through the hole from the inside of the cap. The stem should snap into place with a snug fit. Now screw the cap onto the bottle.

The 2-liter-bottle rocket is ready for launch. Take the rocket and pump to an open field. Attach the pump to the end of the valve stem and put your safety glasses back on. Pump the rocket to a pressure of 30 pounds per square inch (psi)—about 200 kilopascals (kpl) in metric units. Make sure there are no other people around and aim the rocket away from your face. Quickly release the pump from the valve. The rocket should take off. Did it fly straight or tumble? How does it compare with what your balloon rocket did?

Retrieve the rocket, pressurize it to 60 lb (400 kpl), and again launch it in a safe direction. Be sure to pressurize your rocket to no greater than 90 lb (600 kpl). Ninety pounds is approximately one half the bursting strength of this kind of bottle. A 90-lb limit gives you a safety margin of 2 to 1, which is the minimum engineers typically work with.

Does the rocket travel farther with greater pressure? What can you do to stabilize the rocket so that it flies straight? Design a launch pad that will permit you to launch the rocket while standing several meters away. Also, try different bottle sizes. The bottle cap you modified will also fit on 1- and 3-liter bottles. Is there any difference in performance in the three bottles? Why?

For more information on how to make and use high-performance soft-drink-bottle rockets, look up the following two articles at the library:

1. Hawthorne, M., and G. Saunders. "It's Launchtime!" *Science and Children*, vol. 30, no. 5 (1993), pp. 17–19, 39.

2. Winemiller, J.; J. Pedersen; and R. Bonnstetter. "The Rocket Project." *Science Scope*, vol. 15, no. 2 (1991), pp. 18–22.

If your library doesn't carry these two magazines, your librarian can probably arrange to get them for you.

ROCKET THRUST

The thrust of the bottle rocket in the previous project depended on the amount of air pressure inside. In real rockets, thrust is produced by rocket fuel. How rapidly the rocket accelerates into space depends on the size of the thrust and the mass of the rocket. This is Newton's second law of motion in action.

To understand the second law, think about a cannon shooting a cannonball. When the cannon is fired, an explosion propels a cannonball out the open end of the barrel. The ball may fly a kilometer or two to its target. At the same time the cannon itself may be pushed backward a meter or two. This is Newton's third

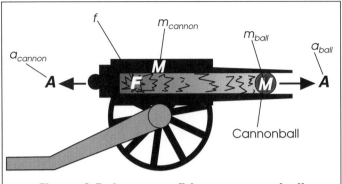

Figure 3-5. A cannon firing a cannonball demonstrates Newton's laws of motion.

law at work; an action produces a reaction. The force acting on the cannon and the ball is the same. But the second law determines what happens to the cannon and the ball as a result of the force. The force accelerates each object in opposite directions according to its mass as shown in Figure 3-5. Newton expressed this relationship in equation form as follows:

$$f = ma$$

where f is the force, m is the mass, and a is the acceleration. Newton's second law is: *Force equals mass times acceleration.*

In the cannon example, the force on the cannon and cannonball are the same, so the equations can be written:

$$f = m_{cannon}a_{cannon}$$
$$f = m_{ball}a_{ball}$$

Thus:

$$m_{cannon}a_{ball} = m_{ball}a_{ball}$$

Because the mass of the cannonball is much smaller than the mass of the cannon, the ball has a much greater acceleration than the cannon. That is why it travels so much farther.

To apply this principle to a rocket, think of the gases being ejected from the rocket engine as the cannon-ball. Think of the rocket as the cannon. The force comes from the controlled explosion taking place inside the rocket's engines. The explosion accelerates the gas one way and the rocket the other.

The following project will help you understand Newton's second law.

Newton Car

Make the Newton car by screwing three wood screws into a large block of wood, as shown in Figure 3-6. Slip a rubber band around the two screws on one end of the block. Pulling both strands of the rubber band back toward the third screw, tie a small loop of string around the rubber band and the screw. Now drill two large holes in one of the long edges of a small wooden block. Hold the block in a vise as you drill, and make each hole large enough to hold two lead fishing sinkers.

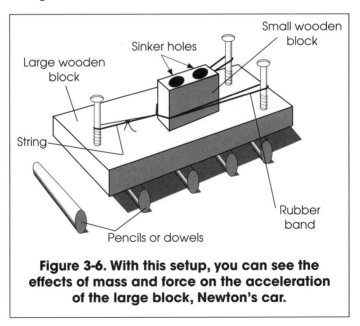

Figure 3-6. With this setup, you can see the effects of mass and force on the acceleration of the large block, Newton's car.

Materials

- Large wooden block, about 10 x 20 x 2.5 cm
- Small wooden block, about 7.5 x 5 x 2.5 cm
- 3 3-in no. 10 wood screws (round head)
- 12 round pencils or short dowels
- 3 rubber bands
- Cotton string
- 4 lead fishing sinkers (about 1/2 ounce each)
- Matches
- Vise
- Screwdriver
- Drill and a bit with larger diameter than the lead sinkers
- Meter stick

Place a dozen round pencils or dowels in a row on a flat surface. They should be separated from each other, much like railroad ties on railroad tracks. Mark the position of each rod so that you can set it up again exactly the same way.

As shown in the illustration, place the large block over part of the row of rods so that the end of the block with two screws is at the end of the row. Slip the small block (without sinkers) into the rubber bands as shown. In preparation for running the test, mark the position of the "car," or large block, with respect to the flat surface.

Now light a match and ignite the ends of the string hanging from the knot in the loop of string. When the string burns through, the rubber band should propel the small block off the car, and the car should roll in the other direction. Measure how far the car travels along the table top.

Set up for another launch using the same string-loop size and the same positioning as before. But this time, add a second rubber band to the two screws. Again, burn the string and measure how far the car travels. Then try it again with three rubber bands. Next, go back to one rubber band, but add two sinkers to the small block. Follow with two and then three rubber bands. Finally, repeat the experiments one more time with four sinkers in the holes in the small block.

Plot the data from each experiment on a bar graph. Put the number of rubber bands or the sinkers on the horizontal, or X axis, of the graph, and plot the distance the car traveled along the vertical, or Y axis.

Which car traveled farther, the car with one rubber band or with three rubber bands? The car with no sinkers in the small block or the car with four sinkers? The rubber bands accelerate the small block, throwing it off the car. When you add rubber bands, you increase the acceleration of the small block and consequently, the force on the large block. When you add sinkers, you increase the mass of the small block. The distance the car travels reflects the effect of these changes on the car. Do you see how Newton's second law applies to this experiment?

The principle behind the Newton car is the same as the one operating in cannons and rockets, but rockets are different in some ways. With the car and cannon, the thrust lasts for just a moment. The thrust in a rocket continues as long as its engines fire, usually until it reaches orbit.

Furthermore, the mass of the rocket changes during flight. A rocket includes engines, propellant tanks, a payload, a control system, and propellants. By far, the largest part of the rocket's mass is its propellants. But the propellant mass steadily declines as the engines fire, reducing overall rocket mass. According to Newton's second law, the acceleration of the rocket must increase as its mass decreases if the thrust remains the same. That is why a rocket starts off moving slowly and goes faster and faster as it climbs into space.

Newton's second law is especially useful for designing efficient rockets. To enter low Earth orbit, it is necessary for a rocket not only to reach the proper altitude, but also to attain a speed in excess of 28,000 km/hr (17,391 mi/hr). A speed of over 40,250 km/hr (24,232 mi/hr), called the *escape velocity*, enables a rocket to escape Earth's gravitational field and travel out into deep space. To reach these high velocities efficiently, rocket engines must be able to burn large masses of fuel very rapidly. Only then will the thrust be great enough to produce the necessary rocket acceleration.

Applied to rocket engines, Newton's second law of motion can be restated in the following way: The greater the mass of rocket fuel burned, and the faster the gas accelerates from the engine, the greater the thrust of the rocket.

Knowing Newton's second law, what might you do to improve the flight of the soft-drink-bottle rocket? If you can, get a toy water rocket from a toy store. Try flying the rocket with and without water and compare the altitude it achieves. How does Newton's second law apply here?

The efficiency of a rocket can be improved by dropping fuel tanks when they become empty. This principle is known as rocket staging. Do you see how this is a practical application of Newton's second law of motion? Rocket staging can be demonstrated with two long balloons.

Balloon Staging

You will need an assistant for this experiment. You will mount balloons on a fishing line stretched across a room. First, thread the fishing line through two plastic straws laid end to end and then secure the line to opposite walls so that it is taut.

Now cut off the bottom half of a paper coffee cup, leaving a paper ring. After inflating the two balloons a bit to stretch them, inflate one balloon about three fourths full of air and squeeze its opening, or nozzle, closed. Stretch the nozzle of the balloon through the inside of the coffee cup ring while your helper inflates the other balloon inside the ring. Your helper's balloon

---

Materials

- 2 oblong balloons
- Paper or Styrofoam coffee cup
- Monofilament fishing line
- Two plastic soft-drink straws
- Masking tape

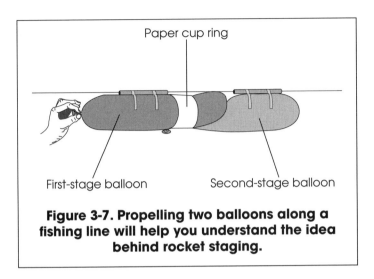

Paper cup ring

First-stage balloon   Second-stage balloon

Figure 3-7. Propelling two balloons along a fishing line will help you understand the idea behind rocket staging.

should fit inside the ring as shown in Figure 3-7. As this balloon inflates, it should press against the nozzle of the other balloon and take over the job of holding it shut. It may take a few tries to accomplish this. Once you have, your assistant should continue squeezing the nozzle of his or her balloon closed.

Tape each balloon to a straw as shown in the illustration. Try to align the long axis of the balloons as closely as possible with the fishing line. Move them to one end of the line, and then have your assistant release the balloon. Watch the escaping gas propel both balloons along the fishing line. When one balloon runs out of air, the other balloon should open and continue the trip.

You may have to try several launchings before you get the second, "upper-stage" balloon to travel completely across the room. Once you do, try other arrangements such as three balloon stages and placing the balloons side by side. Can you fly a two-stage balloon without the fishing line as a guide? How could you modify the balloons to make this possible? Why do rockets that go into outer space have multiple stages? What are the stages on the space shuttle?

4

MODEL ROCKETRY

The most exciting way to experiment with rockets is to use model rockets. Model rocketry is an international sport that millions of people enjoy. High-performance rocket engines and rocket body kits are available from toy and hobby stores or from catalogs.

Never try to make your own rocket engines. It is one of the most dangerous things you can do. Until safe model rockets were invented in the 1950s, many people lost eyes, fingers, and even their lives to homemade rocket engines that exploded prematurely. Commercial engines are safe and provide precise thrusts. They can propel your rockets with payloads to altitudes of hundreds and even thousands of meters above the ground.

Model rocket companies sell many precut kits for rocket bodies. Some are designed for show, some replicate NASA and military rockets, and others are designed for high-performance flight. If you are a beginner, start with a kit to learn the basics. Be sure to follow the instructions, especially those on how to streamline the rocket. Rockets with crooked fins and rough surfaces generate a great deal of drag as they

A model rocket blasts off.

fly through the air. This greatly reduces their performance and the altitude they reach.

After you've had some experience with model rocketry, try designing your own rockets. One of the most important things to consider is the stability of the rocket. You want your rocket to travel straight up rather than tumble through the air. Unless it is stabilized, any object in flight tends to tumble.

The stability of a rocket depends on the location of its *center of mass*. The center of mass is the point along the length of the rocket where the mass to either side of the point is equivalent. You can easily find the center of mass of an object such as a ruler by balancing it on your finger. If the ruler is of uniform thickness and density, the center of mass should be exactly halfway down the stick. If a heavy nail were driven into one of its ends, the center of mass would shift toward the end with the nail.

A rocket with a center of mass far from its nose tends to be unstable. Any slight force on the nose could cause the rocket to begin tumbling around its center of mass. Think of the rocket as a lever with a fulcrum at the center of mass. If the distance from the fulcrum to the nose is long, it takes only a small force to get the rocket rotating. That is why a steady, precise thrust is important in a rocket; any sudden change in thrust could destabilize it.

In space rockets, a control system helps minimize unstable motions by adjusting the engine thrust to oppose them whenever they arise. Model rockets don't have these control systems, so it is very important to design the rocket body so that the center of mass is as close as possible to the nose.

When rocket designers talk about unstable motions of the nose, they specify them as a *pitch* or a *yaw*. In an orbiting rocket, a pitch is an up-and-down movement of the nose, and a yaw is a sideways movement of the nose. Any movement in either of these two directions can cause the rocket to go off course. Since these movements are rotations about the center of mass, the pitch and yaw axes intersect at this point, as shown in Figure 4-1. A rocket can also *roll* about its center axis, but this motion actually helps to stabilize the rocket, just as it helps to roll, or spiral, a football when you throw it.

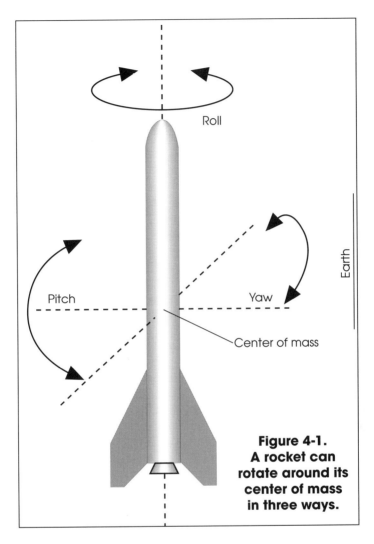

**Figure 4-1.
A rocket can
rotate around its
center of mass
in three ways.**

Another factor in the stability of a rocket is the location of its *center of pressure*. It is the point along the rocket at which the area of the rocket's outer surface to one side of the point is equal to the surface area to the other side. The center of pressure is important because air flowing past the moving rocket rubs and pushes against the outer surface of the rocket. The air

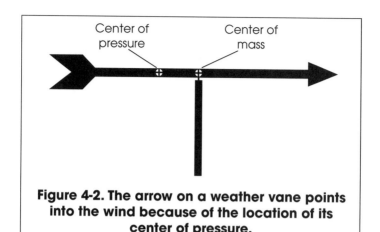

Figure 4-2. The arrow on a weather vane points into the wind because of the location of its center of pressure.

exerts pressure, or force per unit area; the greater the surface area, the greater the force. The surface area should be greater near the tail than near the nose so that the nose stays pointed in the direction of flight.

The same principle ensures that the arrow of a weather vane always points into the wind. Think for a moment of a weather vane like the one shown in Figure 4-2. Designed to indicate wind direction, the arrow rotates freely around a vertical rod mounted on a rooftop. The arrow is balanced so that its center of mass coincides with the rod, or the pivot point.

But the tail of the arrow has a much larger surface area than the arrowhead; in other words, the center of pressure is closer to the tail. As a result, the flowing air imparts a greater force to the tail than the head, and so pushes the tail away. The arrow rotates so that its head points into the oncoming wind and the tail points downwind. If the center of pressure were in the same place as the center of mass, then the wind would favor neither end. Instead of pointing, the arrow would wobble around on its pivot.

For similar reasons, it is extremely important that the center of pressure in a rocket be located toward the tail and the center of mass be located toward the nose. If they are in the same place or too close to each other, then the rocket will be unstable in flight. Its nose would have a greater tendency to wobble, producing a dangerous situation.

You can test your rockets for stability before flight by placing them in a wind tunnel. A controlled stream of air flows through the tunnel and around the rocket, simulating what the rocket will encounter as it flies through the air. Rocket and airplane designers use wind tunnels to test their designs under controlled conditions.

Rocket Wind Tunnel

You can make a wind tunnel out of a cardboard wardrobe box. Begin by laying the box on its side and removing both ends. About one quarter of the way from one end of the box, stack paper towel tubes so that they are aligned along the length of the box as shown in Figure 4-3. Fill the cross section of the box with tubes, packing them closely in a regular pattern like a honeycomb, and then glue them together. These tubes

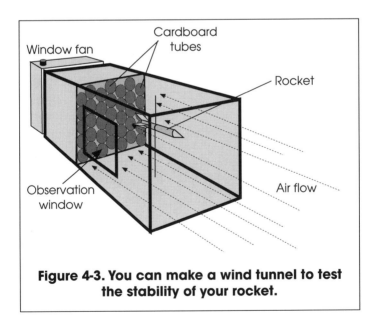

Figure 4-3. You can make a wind tunnel to test the stability of your rocket.

—51—

will help make air flowing into the tunnel travel in straight lines. If they are arranged irregularly, they will not produce an even airflow. Are there other ways you could control the airflow without using tubes?

Near the other end of the box, cut a window in one of the sides as shown in the figure. You will suspend your rocket in the middle of the box's cross section directly in front of this window. First, prepare the rocket for flight, inserting a new engine and packing any payloads and a parachute or other recovery system. Now find its center of mass by balancing it on your finger. Wrap a heavy rubber band snugly around the rocket at its center of mass.

Tie a piece of fishing line to the rubber band on top of the rocket, and tie another fishing line directly opposite it on the bottom. With duct tape or staples, attach the top line to the top of the box and attach the bottom line to the bottom of the box, pulling both lines relatively taut. Cover the window with a piece of plastic wrap and tape it in place.

Place a large window fan against the open end of the box near the stack of tubes. Position the fan facing outward so that it blows air away from the tunnel. This will draw air into the tunnel from the other side. If your rocket is stable in flight, its nose cone should point away from the fan and the tubes. If the rocket is not very stable, it should wobble or turn in the wrong direction. That means it's probably time to go back to the old drawing board. Or it could mean that the air flow through your tunnel is not uniform. Irregular honey-

Materials

- Large window fan
- Cardboard wardrobe box (available from moving companies)
- Tubes from paper towel or toilet paper rolls
- Cellophane tape
- Clear plastic wrap
- Lightweight monofilament fishing line
- White glue
- Sharp knife
- Heavy rubber band

combs of tubes or glue may block or reroute the air-flow. You may have to experiment with several different honeycombs to get the strong, even airflow necessary for wind tunnel tests.

If your rocket is stable, take it out for launch. If it is not, you must increase its stability. You might try adding fins or making them larger to increase the surface area at the tail. But be careful not to shift the center of mass too far from the nose of the rocket!

OTHER MODEL ROCKETRY PROJECTS

● Getting your rocket back for future flights is just as important as launching it. Most model rocket kits include parachutes to bring rockets back down safely. Go to the library and look up information on other methods of rocket recovery. If you want a challenge, try designing a recovery system for your rocket. Some of the possibilities are gliding recovery, which the space shuttle uses; auto rotation, in which rotating helicopter blades land the craft; and a system that generates hang glider wings during landing.

If you plan to launch a payload with your rocket, how can you protect it when it lands? A good way to test your design before the flight is to try it on a raw egg dropped from a second-story window onto a hard sur-face. Can you design a package that will prevent the egg from breaking on impact?

● Try other model rocketry projects such as flying multistage vehicles and designing payloads. Rocket cameras are available from some model rocket com-panies. They can take high-altitude pictures of your neighborhood. A series of high-altitude pictures of your school neighborhood would make an excellent sci-ence fair project, if you include aerial and spacecraft pictures of the same area for comparison.

Altitude Tracking by Time

An interesting part of model rocketry is tracking the vehicle and determining how high it flies. Model rockets can reach hundreds of meters in altitude, so tracking them can be quite a challenge. You could estimate a rocket's altitude by measuring the time it takes to fall back to Earth, but your estimate would be very rough. Furthermore, this method works only with rockets that have no recovery system to slow the fall. Such rockets are destroyed on impact.

To determine altitude by the falling method, you must determine when the rocket reaches the top of its flight. You will need a pair of binoculars to see exactly when the rocket heels over and starts coming back down. Then measure the time to impact in seconds. When you have an answer, let's say 5 s, calculate the altitude with the following equation:

Materials

- Stop watch or watch with second hand
- Binoculars (optional)

$$d = \frac{1}{2} at^2$$

In this equation, d is the distance the rocket fell; a is the acceleration of gravity, 9.8 m/s^2; and t is the falling time. Substituting the values, we get:

$$d = \frac{1}{2} \times 9.8 \, \frac{m}{s^2} \times (5 \, s)^2$$

$$d = \frac{1}{2} \times 9.8 \, m \times 5^2 = 4.9 \, m \times 25 = 120 \, m$$

The rocket reached an altitude of 120 m. However, because it is tricky pinpointing exactly when the rocket starts falling back to Earth, the altitude estimate is rough, to say the least. The estimate does not take into account air friction, which slightly brakes the rocket's fall. Since the falling time is longer than the time it would take the rocket to fall in a vacuum, the estimate is greater than the actual altitude. Can you think of any other sources of error in this method?

A much more accurate method for determining rocket altitude relies on trigonometry. This branch of

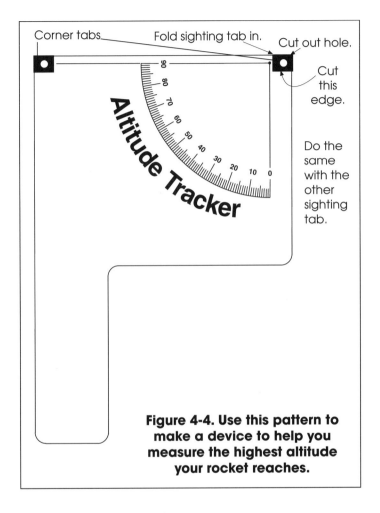

Corner tabs

Fold sighting tab in.

Cut out hole.

Cut this edge.

Do the same with the other sighting tab.

Altitude Tracker

90 80 70 60 50 40 30 20 10 0

Figure 4-4. Use this pattern to make a device to help you measure the highest altitude your rocket reaches.

mathematics sets out the proportions between the sides and angles in right triangles. You can easily calculate your rocket's altitude by considering it to be one leg of a giant triangle.

Altitude Tracking With Trigonometry

First, you must construct a simple altitude tracker. Take this book to a copier store and ask the operator to copy Figure 4-4, the altitude tracker pattern, onto

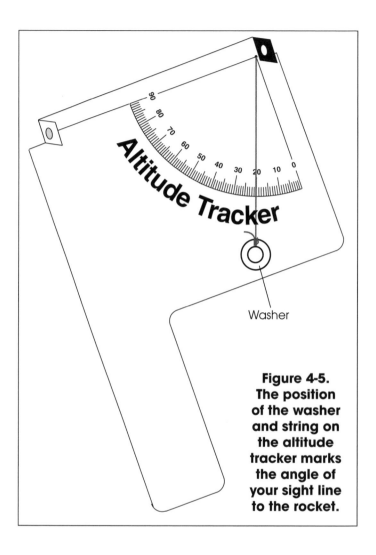

Washer

**Figure 4-5.
The position
of the washer
and string on
the altitude
tracker marks
the angle of
your sight line
to the rocket.**

heavyweight paper. Also specify that the pattern be
enlarged 200 percent. Then cut out the tracker pattern
from the heavy paper. Punch or cut the holes in the
corner tabs and cut across the bottom edges of the
tabs. Fold the two tabs toward each other on the
printed side as shown in Figure 4-5.

Tie a small washer to a short length of string. Punch a small hole at the corner of the protractor and thread the string through the hole. Knot the string on the other side. The string and washer become a plumb that can measure angles in a vertical plane. The holes in the corner tabs are sights you can look through to aim the tracker at the object you want to measure.

Point the tracker at the top of some tall object. The position of the string on the protractor scale gives the angle between the ground and your sight line to the top of the object. This angle is part of a giant triangle consisting of the sight line, the line along the ground to the base of the object, and the object itself. It is a right triangle, since the angle between the object and the ground

Materials
• Tracker pattern
• String
• Washer
• Scissors
• Nail or other sharp, pointed tool
• Tape measure

is 90 degrees. If you know the distance, *b*, from where you're standing to the base of the object, you can calculate the object's height, *h*, according to the following formula:

$h = b \times \tan a$

where *a* is the angle and "tan" is the trigonometric function *tangent*. For any given angle, the function gives the ratio between the two short legs of a right triangle containing the angle. You can look up the tangent of any angle in the trigonometric function table at the end of this project.

You can measure the altitude of your rocket's flight as shown in Figure 4-6. Before launch, lay out the base of your triangle from the launch site to where you will be tracking the rocket from. This baseline should be about 30 m long and should be aligned with the direction the wind is blowing. In other words, the rocket launch site should be 30 m upwind from the tracking site.

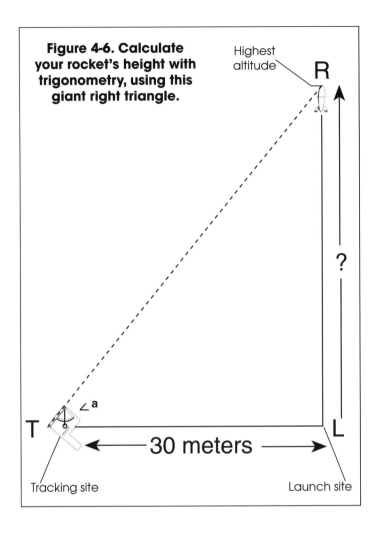

Figure 4-6. Calculate your rocket's height with trigonometry, using this giant right triangle.

Highest altitude

R

?

∠ a

T

← 30 meters →

L

Tracking site

Launch site

The wind can cause the rocket to veer off course, distorting the triangle shape. If your baseline is at an angle to the wind, the distortion can cause your calculation to be way off. But if the launch site is directly upwind from you, the rocket will veer away from you into the wind. As the rocket slows down at the top of its climb, the wind tends to blow it back over the launch site. If this happens, you will get an accurate reading of its altitude. Be sure to keep constant track of the wind because it can change direction just before the launch.

When the rocket is launched, sight the rocket at its highest point. Carefully read the angle of the string and write it down. To calculate the rocket's altitude, use the following formula:

$$RL = LT \times \tan \angle a$$

If your angle is 45 degrees, the tangent is 1.0, and your calculation would look like this:

$$RL = 30 \text{ m} \times 1.0 = 30 \text{ m}$$

There is one other step in the calculation. You must add the height of the tracker device from the ground at the time the measurement was made. Why is this necessary? What would the altitude of the rocket be if the angle were 57 degrees?

You can improve your tracking accuracy by adding another tracking site. Extend your baseline an equal distance on the opposite side of the launch site from the first tracking site. Have an assistant with a second altitude tracker measure the rocket altitude from this site at the same time you measure it from the first site. Average the two angles and again solve for line RL. Why does averaging increase the accuracy of the measurement?

You can get an even greater improvement in accuracy by placing the two baselines at an angle to each other as shown in Figure 4-7. In this case, you must use the following equations to calculate the altitude:

Tracking Station 1 Equation

$$h = \sin A_1 \tan D_2 \frac{b}{\sin (180° - (A_1 + A_2))}$$

Tracking Station 2 Equation

$$h = \sin A_2 \tan D_1 \frac{b}{\sin (180° - (A_1 + A_2))}$$

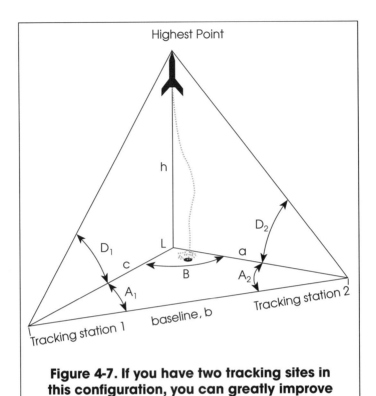

Highest Point

h

D₂

D₁   L

c   B   a

A₁   A₂

Tracking station 2

Tracking station 1

baseline, b

Figure 4-7. If you have two tracking sites in this configuration, you can greatly improve the accuracy of your height measurement.

"Sin" is the abbreviation for *sine*, another trigonometric function that you can look up in the table. Compare your answers for both tracking stations. If the answers are no more than 10 percent apart, you have a good measure of the rocket's altitude.

An advantage of this method is that you can measure the direction the rocket travels, as well as its altitude. If it veers from a vertical path, you will be able to detect it. Your altitude tracker measures only the vertical angle, however. Design a tracking device that measures both the altitude and the horizontal, or *azimuth*, angle at once.

TRIGONOMETRIC FUNCTIONS

Angle	Sine	Cosine	Tangent	Angle	Sine	Cosine	Tangent
1	.0175	.9998	.0175	46	.7193	.6947	1.0355
2	.0349	.9994	.0349	47	.7314	.6820	1.0724
3	.0523	.9986	.0524	48	.7431	.6691	1.1106
4	.0698	.9976	.0699	49	.7547	.6561	1.1504
5	.0872	.9962	.0875	50	.7660	.6428	1.1918
6	.1045	.9945	.1051	51	.7771	.6293	1.2349
7	.1219	.9925	.1228	52	.7880	.6157	1.2799
8	.1392	.9903	.1406	53	.7986	.6018	1.3270
9	.1564	.9977	.1584	54	.8090	.5878	1.3764
10	.1736	.9848	.1763	55	.8192	.5736	1.4281
11	.1908	.9816	.1944	56	.8290	.5592	1.4826
12	.2079	.9781	.2126	57	.8387	.5446	1.5399
13	.2250	.9744	.2309	58	.8480	.5299	1.6003
14	.2419	.9703	.2493	59	.8572	.5150	1.6643
15	.2588	.9659	.2679	60	.8660	.5000	1.7321
16	.2756	.9613	.2867	61	.8746	.4848	1.8040
17	.2924	.9563	.3057	62	.8829	.4695	1.8807
18	.3090	.9511	.3249	63	.8910	.4540	1.9626
19	.3256	.9455	.3443	64	.8988	.4384	2.0503
20	.3420	.9397	.3640	65	.9063	.4226	2.1445
21	.3584	.9336	.3839	66	.9135	.4067	2.2460
22	.3746	.9272	.4040	67	.9205	.3907	2 3559
23	.3907	.9205	.4245	68	.9272	.3746	2.4751
24	.4067	.9135	.4452	69	.9336	.3584	2.6051
25	.4226	.9063	.4663	70	.9397	.3420	2.7475
26	.4384	.8988	.4877	71	.9455	.3256	2.9042
27	.4540	.8910	.5095	72	.9511	.3090	3.0777
28	.4695	.8829	.5317	73	.9563	.2924	3.2709
29	.4848	.8746	.5543	74	.9613	.2756	3.4874
30	.5000	.8660	.5774	75	.9659	.2588	3.7321
31	.5150	.8572	.6009	76	.9703	.2419	4.0108
32	.5299	.8480	.6249	77	.9744	.2250	4.3315
33	.5446	.8387	.6494	78	.9781	.2079	4.7046
34	.5592	.8290	.6745	79	.9816	.1908	5.1446
35	.5736	.8192	.7002	80	.9848	.1736	5.6713
36	.5878	.8090	.7265	81	.9877	.1564	6.3138
37	.6018	.7986	.7536	82	.9903	.1392	7.1154
38	.6157	.7880	.7813	83	.9925	.1219	8.1443
39	.6293	.7771	.8098	84	.9945	.1045	9.5144
40	.6428	.7660	.8391	85	.9962	.0872	11.4301
41	.6561	.7547	.8693	86	.9976	.0698	14.3007
42	.6691	.7431	.9004	87	.9986	.0523	19.0811
43	.6820	.7314	.9325	88	.9994	.0349	28.6363
44	.6947	.7193	.9657	89	.9998	.0175	57.2900
45	.7071	.7071	1.000	90	1.0000	.0000	

5

IN ORBIT

How does a satellite stay in space? If you posed that question to your friends, you would get some pretty strange and funny answers. The typical answer is that there is no gravity in space. If that's true, then why doesn't the satellite just fly off into space and never come back? What holds it in Earth orbit?

Other popular explanations for how satellites stay in space are: the rocket engines keep firing; the satellite flies on the edge of Earth's atmosphere; the satellite flies in a place between Earth and the moon where their gravities cancel out. Part of the confusion people have about satellites and gravity is that they have seen movies of astronauts floating about in their spacecraft. It certainly looks as if there is no gravity in space. But looks can be deceiving.

Earth's gravity does not shut off, as many people believe, when you reach outer space. Remember that Earth's gravity holds the moon in orbit about 400,000 km away—much farther than the beginning of what we consider outer space. So what keeps satellites in orbit? The next project will help answer the question. With this simple demonstration, you can show your friends that the answer to the question is gravity itself.

How does a satellite stay in orbit around Earth?

Satellite Model

With a sharp knife, make a small cut in the side of an old tennis ball. Knot one end of a 2-m-long string and push the knot through the hole in the ball. If you want to make sure the knot doesn't escape, glue the hole shut. Tie the other end of the string to an overhead

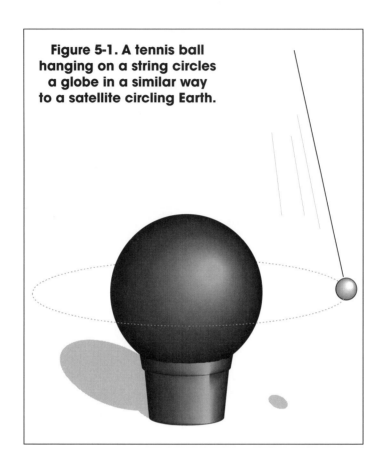

Figure 5-1. A tennis ball hanging on a string circles a globe in a similar way to a satellite circling Earth.

light fixture, tree branch, or some other high object. On the ground below, rest a basketball or a globe of the world in an open coffee can or flowerpot, as shown in Figure 5-1. The center of the globe should be directly underneath the string's attachment point, and the tennis ball should rest alongside the globe at its equator.

Pull the ball straight out from the globe's center and release it. What happens? The ball and string become a pendulum that swings toward the center of the globe. Since the ball is always drawn to the center of the globe, the setup simulates the gravitational pull of Earth on a satellite.

Did your tennis-ball satellite orbit Earth when you released it? What can you do to make it orbit the globe? Try moving the ball in different directions. What happens to the orbit when you move the ball very fast? When you move it slowly? Why does the satellite eventually stop orbiting? While the satellite is orbiting the globe, cut the string to simulate what would happen if gravity disappeared.

Materials
● World globe or basketball
● Old tennis ball
● 2-m-long string
● Sharp knife
● Flower pot

This activity may help you to see that satellites are actually continually falling when they orbit Earth. Newton hypothesized more than 300 years ago that a satellite in constant freefall could orbit Earth. He explained how it would work by imagining a cannon firing cannonballs from the top of a very tall mountain, as shown in Figure 5-2. To avoid having to consider the effects of air friction, he stipulated that the mountain rise high above Earth's atmosphere. The cannon on the mountaintop would fire cannonballs horizontally—to the right in the illustration. As each cannonball was propelled forward, Earth's gravity would pull it toward Earth's surface, transforming its straight-line travel into an arc.

If the cannon were loaded with more black powder each time it was fired, the cannonballs would start at higher and higher velocities. They would travel farther and farther from the mountain before falling to Earth. Soon, the cannonballs would disappear over the horizon. Eventually, if a cannonball were fired with enough energy, it would "fall" entirely around Earth and come back to its starting point. Since it would have the same velocity it started with, it would then continue circling Earth in an orbit.

This is how orbiting spacecraft, such as the space shuttle, stay in orbit. Instead of being launched from a mountain, an orbiter is launched upward from Earth's surface in an arc. The trajectory is designed so that just

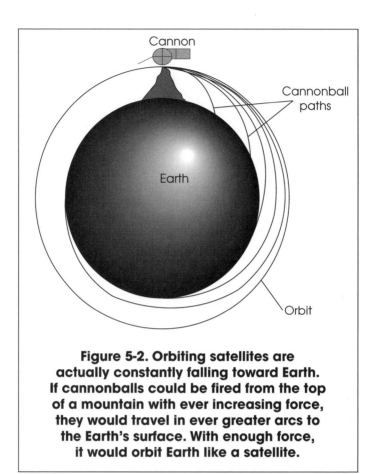

**Figure 5-2. Orbiting satellites are
actually constantly falling toward Earth.
If cannonballs could be fired from the top
of a mountain with ever increasing force,
they would travel in ever greater arcs to
the Earth's surface. With enough force,
it would orbit Earth like a satellite.**

as the orbiter reaches the top of its ascent and becomes horizontal, it is traveling at the right velocity and at the right altitude to keep it continually "falling." For example, if the shuttle climbs to a 320-km-high orbit, it must travel at a speed of about 27,740 km/hr to achieve a stable orbit. At that speed and altitude, the shuttle's falling path will be parallel to the curvature of Earth.

So, hard as it is to believe, the shuttle and the astronauts inside are falling together around Earth. That's why it appears that the astronauts are weightless. Any objects that fall together seem to be weightless with respect to each other. Imagine jumping off a cliff into a river and releasing a rock from your hand in midair. The rock would seem to float in the air next to you. You'll explore this phenomenon further in the next chapter.

Now that you have some basic understanding of orbits, you are ready to calculate some of the parameters of orbital dynamics. For example, if you know a satellite's altitude, you can determine the time it takes to complete one orbit. This orbital period, p, can be calculated using the following equation:

$$p = 2\pi \sqrt{\frac{r^3}{kM}}$$

where r is the distance from the center of Earth to the satellite. M is the mass of Earth, and k is known as the gravitational constant. The product kM, which is found in many orbital equations, is a constant equal to 3.99×10^{14} m^3/sec^2.

Suppose you wanted to calculate the period of a satellite orbiting Earth at an altitude of 352 km (3.52×10^6 m). The value of r would be equal to the altitude of the satellite plus the radius of Earth, which is 3.21×10^6 m; thus, r equals 6.73×10^6 m. To calculate p:

$$p = 2(3.14) \sqrt{\frac{(6.73 \times 10^6)^3}{3.99 \times 10^{14}}}$$

Simplifying the expression, we have:

$$p = 2(3.14)(6.73) \sqrt{\frac{6.73}{3.99}} \times 10^2 = 5{,}490 \text{ s} = 91.5 \text{ minutes}$$

You can also determine the velocity of the satellite using the following equation:

$$v = \sqrt{\frac{kM}{r}} = \sqrt{\frac{3.99 \times 10^{14}}{6.73 \times 10^6}} = 7{,}710 \text{ m/sec}$$

7,710 m/sec = 7.71 km/sec = 27,700 km/hr

The space shuttle flew mission STS-60 in early 1994 at an altitude of 352 km. Thus, it orbited Earth at 27,700 km/hr in less than 92 minutes. You can plot the trajectory of this shuttle's launch in the next project.

Shuttle Launch Trajectory

You can plot the trajectory of the space shuttle if you know its altitude and the horizontal distance traveled at various points in time. The table below contains data supplied by NASA for mission STS-60. For every 10 s during the shuttle's launch, the table gives the altitude in meters and distance in kilometers from the launch pad. The data covers the first 8.5 minutes of flight, until it reaches orbit. That's when the orbiter's main engines shut off and the external tank is dropped.

ALTITUDE AND DISTANCE DATA FOR SHUTTLE MISSION STS-60

Time, in seconds	Altitude, in meters	Surface Range, in kilometers	Time, in seconds	Altitude, in meters	Surface Range, in kilometers
0	0	0.00	270	107,482	291.90
10	259	0.00	280	109,357	315.00
20	612	0.20	290	110,782	342.60
30	2,709	0.90	300	111,932	370.00
40	4,839	2.20	310	112,836	397.90
50	7,465	3.90	320	113,506	248.10
60	10,745	6.30	330	113,946	459.90
70	14,237	9.10	340	114,166	492.30
80	18,733	13.00	350	114,196	526.50
90	24,056	18.00	360	114,048	562.60
100	30,032	24.10	370	113,739	604.10
110	36,569	32.20	380	113,301	658.80
120	43,508	43.10	390	112,741	682.00
130	50,216	53.90	400	112,108	725.30
140	56,536	65.10	410	111,488	771.40
150	62,611	77.60	420	110,710	819.30
160	68,258	90.50	430	110,020	869.80
170	73,548	103.80	440	109,395	922.20
180	78,507	118.40	450	108,879	977.50
190	83,120	134.00	460	108,523	1,036.2
200	87,287	150.10	470	108,363	1,096.7
210	90,802	167.50	480	108,414	1,160.6
220	94,700	185.60	490	108,756	1,227.6
230	97,913	205.40	500	109,344	1,297.3
240	100,805	225.00	510	110,329	1,369.0
250	103,409	249.70	515	110,827	1,409.7
260	105,662	268.60			

Using graph paper, make a graph with distance along the X axis and altitude along the Y axis. Think of the shuttle's launch pad as being located at the intersection of the X and Y axes of the graph. Because the shuttle travels much farther along the surface than it does upward by the time it reaches orbit, the scale on each axis will probably have to be differ-

Materials

- Graph paper
- Ruler
- Pencil or marker pen

ent. A square on the vertical scale might equal 2,500 m while the same square on the horizontal scale might equal 25 km. You will have to decide what scales to use based on the size and number of lines on your graph paper.

Look at the shape of the ascent trajectory of the shuttle. How does it relate to the path of the tennis ball in the previous project and the path of the cannonball in Figure 5-2? What would happen to the shape of the ascent trajectory if you used the same scales for both the X and Y axes?

It should be clear by now that gravity is responsible for keeping a satellite in orbit. Earth and the satellite pull on each other with a force that is directly proportional to the product of their masses. And the farther they are from each other, the smaller the force. The following equation represents this relationship:

$$G = k \sqrt{\frac{m_e m_s}{d^2}}$$

G is the total gravitational force the two objects exert on each other. The values m_e and m_s are the mass of Earth and the mass of the satellite, respectively. The distance between the center of Earth and the center of the satellite is d, and k, the gravitational constant, is equal to 6.67×10^{-11} newton-meter^2/kg^2.

When the satellite is sitting on Earth's surface, we say that the force of gravity is 1 g, or 1 gravity. When the satellite is farther from Earth's center, G is less. For example, if a satellite is orbiting Earth at a distance equal to twice Earth's radius, the gravitational force felt by the satellite is one quarter as great as the force felt at Earth's surface. That's because when d is multiplied by two in the equation, the two becomes squared, and since it is in the denominator, it results in a factor of one fourth. If the satellite were orbiting at a distance of three times Earth's radius, then the value of G would be one ninth as great.

As an interesting activity, make a graph showing this relationship. Plot distances for 1, 2, 3, 4, and 5 times the distance from Earth along the X axis of the graph and the relative strength of the gravitational pull along the Y axis.

You can use the following equation to determine the difference in G at any distance from Earth's center. It is a simplification of the previous equation; see whether you can derive it from that equation.

$$G_s = \sqrt{\frac{R^2}{r^2}} \times G_e$$

G_s is the gravitational pull felt by the satellite in orbit, and G_e is the gravitational pull at the surface of Earth. R is the radius of Earth (6,378 km), and r is the distance between the satellite and the center of Earth.

Use the equation to determine the gravitational force on the following satellites:

SATELLITE	ALTITUDE
A	On Earth's surface
B	100 km high
C	300 km high
D	6,378 km high

Remember that r is the height of the satellite above Earth's center, not just above Earth's surface.

Is there any distance for which the value of G_s is 0? Why, or why not? Will this equation work for any other planet besides Earth?

A spacecraft that escapes orbit travels in a straight line if it is very far from any large gravity source, such as one of the other planets. If the spacecraft comes near a planet or a moon, the gravity of that body pulls the spacecraft down toward it in a curved path.

This is a demonstration of Newton's first law of motion: *Objects in motion will stay in motion in a straight line unless acted upon by an unbalanced force.* Until the spacecraft encounters a planet's gravity, all the forces acting on it are balanced. The gravity is an unbalanced force that causes it to deviate from its path.

6

WHAT IS
MICROGRAVITY?

Rockets are sent into space for many reasons. They may carry scientific instruments that help scientists study the complex interactions of Earth's atmosphere, oceans, land, energy, and living things. Or the instruments may provide clearer views of distant planets, stars, and galaxies than is possible from the ground. Without the filtering effect of the atmosphere, instruments in space can see *all* the light energy that comes to our planet, not just a portion of the electromagnetic spectrum.

When people are on board, the space flight gives them a view of our home as a planet, as well as a view of other worlds up close. The astronauts may even be able to sample the composition of those worlds, as was the case when the Apollo astronauts landed on the moon.

Space flight also allows scientists to investigate living processes and the fundamental states of matter—solids, liquids, and gases—in the artificial weightlessness of space. Access to this environment benefits many research fields, including materials science, combustion, fluids, and biotechnology. The investigations in this chapter present typical experiments that might be performed aboard the space shuttle.

WHAT IS MICROGRAVITY?

As you learned in Chapter 5, the apparent weightlessness inside the shuttle comes about because it—and everything inside—is falling toward Earth. It does not arise, as most people assume, from a lack of gravity in outer space. In fact, there is no known place that gravity does not exist. The Sun's gravity holds Earth in orbit at a distance of about 150 million km away. Even the Sun's movement through the Milky Way galaxy is controlled by gravity exerted by other solar systems light-years away. And the galaxies themselves exert a pull on each other that shapes the universe. There is no such thing as zero gravity.

Yet *zero g* was the term the space industry originally used to describe the environment inside a spacecraft. Recognizing that term as misleading, many scientists now use the term *microgravity* instead.

A microgravity environment comes about whenever two or more objects are in free fall together. Relative to one another, the objects appear to be weightless. You may have experienced this very briefly if you have ever been in an elevator that dropped suddenly. For that instant, it may have felt as though you could rise off the floor.

Imagine that you are in an elevator standing on a bathroom scale and the cable holding the elevator breaks. You, the bathroom scale, and the elevator are in free fall. What would the dial on the scale read? It would read zero, and you would feel weightless. But gravity would still be pulling on you. When you reached the ground, you would feel your weight again in the sudden stop. The act of falling only made it seem as if gravity had disappeared.

If you want to experience microgravity for yourself, take a tennis ball to a pool with a high dive. After making sure there is a wide area of unoccupied water below, step off the high dive holding the ball in front of your face. When you are in the air, release the ball, and keep your eyes fixed on it during the entire fall. It may take several tries before you coordinate stepping off the high dive with the release of the tennis ball.

What happens to the ball when you release it? Does it fall faster, slower, or keep up with you? What does it teach you about microgravity?

Of course, air friction would throw things off a little. Since you are much larger than the ball, air drag would cause you to drop a tiny bit slower than it would the ball. Thus, air drag introduces a deceleration, an upward acceleration equivalent to that produced by a minuscule force of gravity coming from the sky. The term microgravity acknowledges the existence of this and other tiny forces in free fall. In the shuttle, small thrusts of the engine create tiny forces on objects inside when it turns the vehicle during orbit. And the astronauts themselves send vibrations throughout the vehicle when they move about the cabin, pushing off walls and other parts of the shuttle.

In the next project, you can build a device that gives a clear demonstration of microgravity.

The Microgravity Device

The microgravity device consists of a wooden frame that supports a balloon and a lead fishing sinker, as shown in Figure 6-1. The sinker, which is suspended by rubber bands, holds a sharp pin aimed at the balloon. Can you guess what will happen when the frame is dropped to the floor?

To build the frame, use the illustration as a guide. You may have to get someone to help you saw the wood and to drill several holes. If you can saw and drill the wood yourself, make sure you wear safety glasses when you do it. Cut the wood to the size specified in the materials list. Make a rectangle of the four pieces of wood and attach them at the corners using wood screws. You will first have to drill pilot holes through the

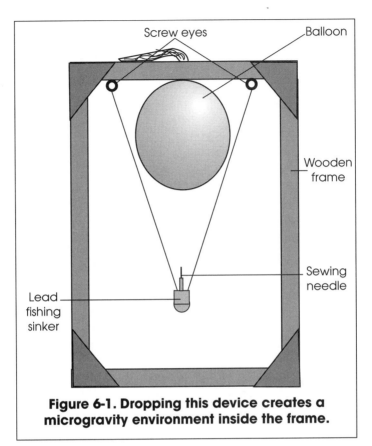

Figure 6-1. Dropping this device creates a microgravity environment inside the frame.

corners. These holes will guide the wood screws as you screw them in.

When the frame is assembled, drill a 1/2-in (12.7-mm) hole through the top piece of wood in the center, at the point where the balloon will be suspended. Also drill pilot holes for two small screw eyes at the positions shown in the illustration. From the inside of the frame, screw a screw eye into each pilot hole. Now with the lead fishing sinker in a vise, drill a small hole in the top of it for inserting the needle or pin.

Make a chain of rubber bands by looping them together end-to-end with slip knots. Attach the fishing sinker to the chain by whatever means are available to attach it to a fishing line. The chain should be just long enough to hang down in the frame as shown in the illustration. Tie each end of the chain to a screw eye mounted in the frame. Glue the eye end of a needle into the hole in the sinker so that the needle stands vertically pointing at the balloon.

Inflate a small round balloon and tie a short piece of string around its opening, or nozzle. Push the string through the hole in the top piece of wood. Pull it tight from the other side so that the balloon is close to the wood, and then tape the string in place to the top of the frame.

Materials

- 2 pieces of wood, 10 x 2 x 1 in
  2 pieces of wood, 15 x 2 x 1 in
- 4 2-in wood screws (#8 or #10)
- Glue
- 2 small screw eyes
- 4 to 6 rubber bands
- 1 6-oz lead fishing sinker
- Long sewing pin or needle
- Small round balloons
- Drill, 1/2-in bit, and bit for pilot holes
- Vise
- Screwdriver
- Masking tape
- Pillow or chair cushion
- Short string

When you have finished making the device, find a place where you can drop it from a height of about 2 m. Position a pillow on the floor at the drop point to cushion the fall. You may want to have an assistant drop the frame so that you can observe closely what happens to the balloon and the pin as it falls. The frame should be held very steady and then released. Did the balloon break? If so, where did it break during its fall? Why?

When the frame is stationary, the weight of the lead fishing sinker stretches the rubber band so that the sinker hangs near the bottom of the frame. Gravity pulls the sinker down while the rubber bands pull it up. When the frame drops, the apparatus is in free fall, resulting in a microgravity environment within the frame. It appears that gravity has been eliminated within the frame: the downward pull on the sinker seems to disappear because the tension in the stretched rubber bands now pulls the sinker upward toward the balloon. The pin should rise high enough to make the balloon pop.

If you are not convinced that the tension in the rubber bands caused the sinker to move toward the balloon, try replacing the rubber bands with a stout string. Repeat the drop test. Does the balloon pop? Now the frame and sinker fall together, and the sinker appears to float in place within the frame; the sinker and frame appear to be weightless relative to each other.

If you have access to a video camera and VCR, you might want to videotape your drop tests and watch them in slow motion. As an added feature of your science project, it will also allow you to determine precisely how far the frame dropped when the balloon popped. When videos are played on the TV screen, they display 30 still pictures per second. Because each successive picture, or frame, varies only slightly from the last, it gives the illusion of a moving image. Play back the drop test in slow motion and count how many frames passed from the moment you dropped the balloon to the moment it popped.

From the number of frames, you can determine how long the sequence was. For example, if the sequence lasted 10 frames, the time elapsed was 10/30 of a second, or about 0.33 s. Calculate the distance the frame dropped with the following formula:

$$d = \frac{1}{2}at^2$$

You may recall this formula from the rocket-tracking activity in Chapter 5: d is the distance the frame falls, a is the acceleration of gravity (9.8 m/s^2), and t is the time.

Falling Water in a Cup

Another way to demonstrate microgravity is to drop a large cup of water from a height of a meter or two.

The trick is to drop the cup upside down and then watch what happens to the water inside. Since the person dropping the cup will not be able to see everything clearly, get an assistant to help you. Take turns dropping the cup so that you both can see what happens.

It is best to do this demonstration outside or on an uncarpeted floor. To catch the water and cup, place a bucket or catch basin on the floor or ground in front of a chair. Fill the cup to the brim with water. Place a cookie sheet on top of the cup and, pressing them together, invert the two. The cup should now be upside down on the cookie sheet.

Stand on the chair and hold the cookie sheet and cup over the bucket at a height of 1 to 2 meters. Gently push the cup to the edge of the sheet. Quickly pull the cookie sheet straight out from under the cup, as shown in Figure 6-2, so that the cup and water are in free fall. Why doesn't the cup tip over when you pull the cookie sheet out from under it?

Materials
• Large clear-plastic beverage cup
• Cookie sheet with no sides, or flat metal sheet
• Water
• Catch basin or bucket
• Chair

Does the water fall out of the cup as soon as the cookie sheet is out of the way? What happens to the water and the cup during the fall? Why? It would be helpful to videotape this demonstration too.

Water usually falls out of a cup when it is turned upside down, but in the special environment of microgravity, the water stays in the cup. That's because the water and the cup fall together, and relative to each other, gravity disappears. However, outside the microgravity environment, you and your assistant can certainly see that gravity is still there because the cup and water are falling.

Microgravity environments exist outside free fall, but they are hard to come by. One such place is the point between Earth and the moon where their gravities

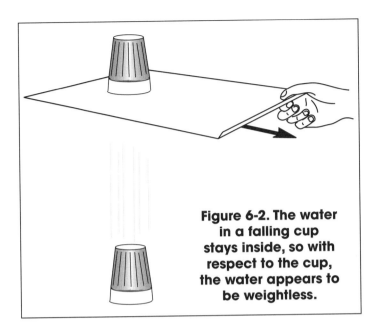

Figure 6-2. The water in a falling cup stays inside, so with respect to the cup, the water appears to be weightless.

cancel out. The gravitational pull along the line between Earth and moon reaches zero at this one point, though there are minuscule gravitational pulls in other directions from the Sun and other sources. Can you figure out where the canceling point is, with the help of a little bit of research? Remember that the gravitational pull of Earth is greater than the moon's, so the canceling point must be closer to the moon than Earth.

Still another microgravity environment is far away from all planets, moons, and stars. At a distance of 6.37 million km from Earth, almost 17 times farther away than the moon, Earth's gravity is only one one-millionth of a g, or 1×10^{-6} g. Just for fun, try to imagine what it would be like if you could go that far out into space. Since gravity is not really eliminated, objects still fall. On Earth, if you jumped off a roof 4.9 m high, it would take you 1 s to reach the ground. How long would it take you to fall 4.9 m if you were in a microgravity environment of

10^{-6} g? Be careful in answering this question. Don't automatically assume it would take you one million times longer to fall the distance.

CREATING MICROGRAVITY

The National Aeronautics and Space Administration (NASA) has a variety of microgravity environments available for scientific research. Earth orbit is the ideal microgravity environment because it can be maintained indefinitely. However, it is very expensive to place experiments in orbit. A basic space shuttle flight costs hundreds of millions of dollars, and as a result, shuttle flights are limited to a few a year. Much less expensive ways of creating microgravity include drop towers and drop tubes, airplanes, and small rockets.

Drop towers and drop tubes create a temporary free fall, much as a falling elevator with a broken cable would. NASA's Lewis Research Center in Cleveland, Ohio, has a drop tower facility that descends into Earth like a mine shaft. The testing tube is 6.1 m in diameter and 132 m deep. Beneath the drop tube is a catch basin filled with polystyrene beads to give the test equipment a soft landing. The 132-m drop creates a microgravity environment for a period of 5.2 s.

The experimental apparatus is placed in a cylindrical or rectangular test container, or vehicle, that can carry weights of up to 450 kg. As the test vehicle is dropped from the top of the tube, cameras within the vehicle record the action and data is radioed to recorders.

Before the drop, the tube is sealed with a large cap from which the test vehicle hangs. Air is pumped out of the tube to obtain a low vacuum with almost no air drag. As a result, air drag decelerates the vehicle only 10^{-5} g or less. That is the maximum level of microgravity in the environment. Scientists rate microgravity environments according to the maximum acceleration produced by the minuscule forces in the environment. That number tells them how close the environment comes to simulating pure weightlessness. A 1/10-g environment,

**Objects falling through this drop tube at NASA's
Lewis Research Center in Ohio experience
more than 5 seconds of microgravity.**

for example, has forces that produce an effect equivalent to one-tenth of Earth's gravity.

A smaller facility for microgravity research is located at the NASA Marshall Space Flight Center in Huntsville, Alabama. It is a 100-m-high, 25.4-cm-diameter drop tube that can achieve microgravity for periods of as long as 4.5 s. Additional drop facilities of different sizes and for different purposes are located at NASA field centers and in other countries. A 490-m vertical mine shaft in Japan has been converted to a drop facility that can achieve a 10^{-5}-g environment for up to 11.7 s.

AIRCRAFT

Airplanes cannot achieve the high-quality microgravity of drop towers and drop tubes because they are never completely in free fall and the air drag is significant. But the microgravity environment in an airplane lasts for periods of about 25 s or longer. Another advantage is that scientists can ride along with their experiments and, if they hope to ride the shuttle someday, learn to work in microgravity. The NASA Johnson Space Center in Houston, Texas, has a KC-135 aircraft that simulates weightlessness for scientific research and for astronaut training. The plane is a Boeing 707 jet with most of its passenger seats removed and padded walls to protect the people inside.

A typical flight lasting two to three hours includes about 40 periods of microgravity. To create microgravity, the plane climbs quickly and then drops, following the parabolic path shown in Figure 6-3. Starting at an altitude of about 7 km above sea level, the plane climbs at a 45-degree angle in a maneuver called *pulling up*. It then loses air speed, arcs over, and descends at a 45-degree angle until it has reached its original altitude. At this point, it levels out, or *pulls out*.

In its parabolic path, the plane travels between altitudes of 7.3 and 10.4 km. During the pull-up and pull-out segments, the crew and the experiments experience

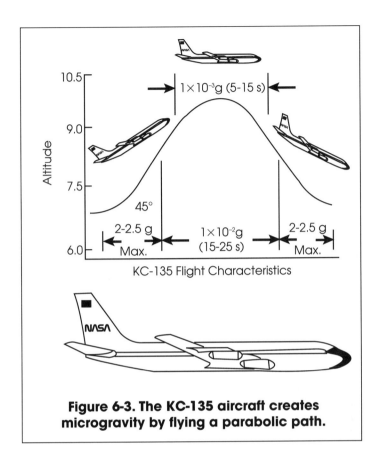

Figure 6-3. The KC-135 aircraft creates microgravity by flying a parabolic path.

between 2 g and 2.5 g. But in between, in the microgravity environment, there are only 10^{-2} g. At the very top of the parabola, g-forces drop as low as 10^{-3} g. The gut-wrenching sensations passengers experience on the flight have earned the plane the nickname of "vomit comet."

You can generate microgravity in a soft-drink can in the same way the KC-135 airplane does.

Microgravity in a Soda-Pop Can

Using a sharp nail, punch a small hole near the bottom of an empty soda-pop can, as shown in Figure 6-4.

Astronaut trainees experience microgravity aboard a KC-135 aircraft.

Fill the can with water, placing your thumb over the hole to keep the water in. Then hold the can over a catch basin and remove your thumb. Water should pour out of the hole. Watch the water as you let the can fall into the basin. What happens to the water stream? Why?

Figure 6-4. Punch a hole near the bottom of an empty soda can, fill it with water, and let it drop. Watch what happens to the water streaming out of the hole.

Now punch a hole in a second empty soda can and fill it with water as you did the first can. Standing a couple of meters away from the catch basin, throw the can up into the air in an arc so that it lands in the basin. (See Figure 6-5.) Try to avoid tumbling or spinning the can in flight. Does the water stream out of the can's hole? Why? Why should you avoid tumbling or spinning the can when you toss it? How do the results of this experiment explain what happens on the KC-135 aircraft?

> *Materials*
>
> • 2 empty soda-pop cans
> • Sharp nail
> • Water
> • Catch basin

ROCKETS

A third technology for creating microgravity is small rockets. These rockets, known as sounding rockets,

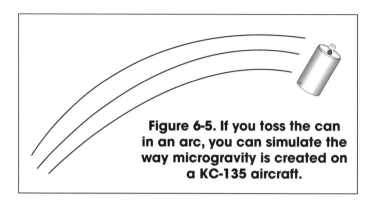

Figure 6-5. If you toss the can in an arc, you can simulate the way microgravity is created on a KC-135 aircraft.

don't go into orbit, but they climb above the atmosphere and then drop, producing several minutes of free fall. This free fall period comes after the fuel has burned out and when the rocket is coasting before it reenters the atmosphere. The rockets usually achieve microgravity at or below 10^{-5} g. NASA uses sounding rockets extensively for microgravity experiments.

It should be clear by now that airplanes, drop facilities, and small rockets share a common problem in creating microgravity environments. After a few seconds or minutes of microgravity, Earth gets in the way and the free fall stops. In spite of this limitation, much can be learned in these microgravity environments about the nature of fluids and mixing, crystallization, and the molecular structure of matter.

But experiments involving slow processes and subtle effects require more time. To conduct long-term experiments lasting days, weeks, months, and years, Earth orbit is the only option. On the space shuttle, a microgravity environment is created from the moment its rocket engines stop firing until it reenters Earth's atmosphere, usually about two weeks after launch.

Because Earth's atmosphere thins out gradually, the shuttle never really operates in a perfect vacuum. Orbiting even hundreds of kilometers from Earth, it collides with atoms of oxygen and nitrogen. Those collisions create g-forces inside of approximately 1×10^{-6} g.

This sounding rocket, called the Black Brant, is one of the vehicles NASA uses to create microgravity.

WEIGHT AND MASS IN SPACE

As you might expect, one of the difficulties with conducting research in the shuttle's microgravity environment is measuring weight. If scientists wanted to periodically weigh the rats in an experiment to see whether they are eating well and staying healthy, how would they do it? In microgravity, spring scales always read zero, and beam balances fail to balance. So instead of measuring weight, scientists are forced to measure mass.

Mass is the quantity of matter an object contains. The object's weight is a force that comes from the pull of gravity on its mass. Weight can be calculated by multiplying the mass by the acceleration of gravity, which is an application of Newton's second law, $F = ma$. So for an object that remains on Earth, its weight and mass always differ by a constant—the acceleration of gravity. In recognition of this fact, weight in the metric system is usually given in kilograms, even though a kilogram is a unit of mass.

Because of the space age, we are now able to go to places where the magnitude of gravity is very different from that on Earth. Trying to use Earth's standard for weight in other worlds is a problem. For example, a person with a mass of 100 kg on Earth has the same mass on the moon, yet a scale would indicate a weight of 16.7 kg on the moon because of the lower gravity.

The following experiment will help you to understand the relationship between mass and weight.

Weight and Mass

Fill a dishwashing detergent bottle to the top with sand. Then add as much water as you can and seal the bottle. Fill an identical bottle with dry sand and seal it. Pick up the bottles, one in each hand, and compare how heavy they feel.

Now place a small amount of liquid soap and water on a smooth countertop and smear it around. This will serve as a lubricant. Place the first bottle on the liquid soap and without lifting it, slide the bottle from side to side over the surface. Move it as quickly as possible. Repeat with the second bottle. If necessary,

Materials
• 2 opaque plastic bottles (dish-detergent bottles) of the same size
• Sand
• Water
• Liquid soap

add more liquid soap to the countertop. Which bottle is easier to accelerate? Compare the ease of acceleration with how heavy they feel. What do you sense as you move the bottles from side to side? Can you think of a way to use this effect to measure mass in microgravity? In performing this test, why is it necessary to place the bottles on a surface?

You should have found that the heavier bottle was harder to accelerate. Because it has more mass, the bottle has more *inertia*, which is an object's resistance to motion. In the next project, you can make a device based on the principle explored in the previous project. It is an inertial balance similar to those used aboard the shuttle to measure mass.

Inertial Balance

Sandwich one end of a metal yardstick between two blocks of wood, as shown in Figure 6-6. Drill two holes through the sandwich and bolt them together. Anchor the wood blocks to a tabletop with C-clamps, letting the other end of the yardstick hang off the table so that it can swing freely from side to side. Tape an empty plastic film canister upright to the free end of the yardstick. You now have a device that will measure the inertia of items placed in the canister. To keep items from moving around in the canister, cut a piece of

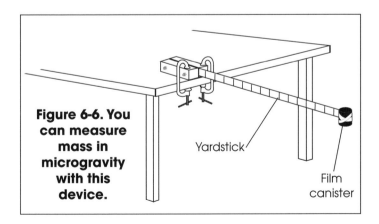

Figure 6-6. You can measure mass in microgravity with this device.

Yardstick

Film canister

foam to fill the inside of the canister and anchor each item with it.

First you must calibrate your inertial balance with an object, such as a penny, that will represent a standard unit of mass. With only the foam plug in the canister, push the free end of the yardstick to one side and release it. Using a stopwatch or a watch with a second hand, time how long it takes the stick to complete 25 cycles of oscillation. A cycle is the movement from one side to the other and back again. Calculate and record the number of cycles per second (cycles/s).

Repeat the measurement with a single penny in the canister. Again, measure the time it takes to complete 25 cycles and record the number of cycles/s. Repeat the procedure a number of times, adding a penny each time until you reach 10 pennies. Plot a graph with the number of cycles/s on the Y axis and the number of pennies on the X axis. The line through your plotted points calibrates your balance in penny units of mass.

Materials

- Metal yardstick or meterstick (available from hardware stores)
- 2 C-clamps
- Plastic 35-mm film canister
- Pillow foam (cut to fit inside canister)
- Masking tape
- 2 wood blocks
- 2 bolts and nuts
- Drill and bit
- Graph paper, ruler, and pencil
- Pennies and nickel
- Stopwatch or watch with a second hand

Place an object of unknown mass, such as a nickel, in the bucket and time 25 cycles. Locate the resulting number of cycles/s on the Y axis and the plotted line of your graph, and read the corresponding number of pennies on the X axis. You now know the mass of the nickel in penny units.

If you want to calibrate your inertial balance in grams, get a metric beam balance and weigh your penny, or any other objects you'd like to use. Your school science lab should have a balance you can borrow. Will an inertial balance work in microgravity? Try to design an inertial balance that will measure the mass of rodents on the space shuttle.

CRYSTALS

One of the most important ways scientists use the microgravity environment on the shuttle is to grow nearly perfect crystals. Crystals form when atoms and molecules line up in a regular pattern in a material changing from liquid to solid. You've probably seen ice crystals form when water freezes in the outdoors. The crystals grow because the molecules keep building on top of each other. Many other solid materials, including salt and sugar, are crystalline.

As crystals grow, gravity sometimes causes defects in the arrangement of the atoms. In microgravity, the crystals grow symmetrically in a regular pattern. Microgravity scientists study such crystals of silicon and other materials to help them better understand their properties. In their experiments to improve the performance of these materials, they need consistent crystal growth to discover how different factors influence crystal properties. It's difficult to get consistent results in gravity because the defects it causes are random.

The size and shape of crystals in steel greatly affect the strength, durability, and flexibility of the material. In studying the growth of these crystals at the atomic level, scientists hope to find ways of growing them that will improve such material properties. They study silicon, a major component of solid-state electronics, in order to make more-efficient electronics. Medical researchers study protein crystals to find ways to modify their shape in the search for new medicines to fight disease.

Crystals grow in solutions in the space shuttle's microgravity environment. A solution is water containing a dissolved solid, such as salt. When there is a large amount of salt dissolved in water, crystals may start to form. If gravity were present, the fluid surrounding each crystal would flow upward because of differences in density

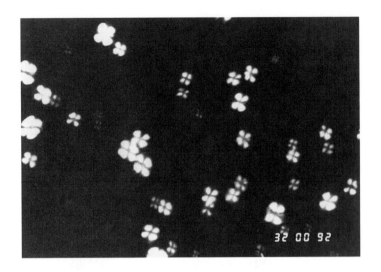

These are protein crystals grown aboard the space shuttle.

within the solution. The fluid next to the crystal surface deposits its dissolved material onto the crystal, thereby reducing the molecular weight of that part of the solution. Since it's lighter, the solution tends to float upward.

This fluid flow can cause defects in the crystal by causing atoms to misalign in the crystal structure. Just one atom out of place for every one million or even one billion atoms properly aligned in a crystal structure can change how the crystal functions. Growing crystals in microgravity during a two-week mission on the space shuttle can yield much larger, more perfect crystals of many substances than is possible on the ground. Later analysis of these crystals tells the scientists what their atomic structure is and provides clues to how to alter the crystals in a controlled way so as to change their properties.

Thus, understanding and controlling solution flows is vital to studies of crystal growth. In the next experiment, you can actually see gravity-driven fluid motion.

Gravity-Driven Fluid Flow

Begin the experiment by filling two large beakers nearly full with water of the same temperature. To ensure that the temperatures in the two beakers are equal, first fill a pitcher with water and stir it for about a minute. Then, transfer the water to the beakers. Pour salt into one of the beakers until the water tastes very salty. The exact amount of salt is not important. Stir the water so that the salt dissolves completely.

Tie threads around two small glass vials near their openings, leaving long tails of thread. Holding a vial by the thread as shown in Figure 6-7, dip it into the salt water and fill it up. Set the vial aside in a stand. Dip the second vial into the fresh water and fill it up. Set it aside also. Be sure to remember which vial is which.

Figure 6-7. Lower a test tube of colored saltwater by a thread into a beaker of water to trigger gravity-driven fluid flow.

When the water has stopped swirling in the beakers, add several drops of food coloring to the vial with fresh water. Sealing the vial with your thumb, shake it to distribute the coloring through the water. The water in the vial should have a deep color that is easy to see.

Holding the vial of colored water by the thread, gently lower it into the beaker of salty water. Let the vial come to rest on the bottom of the beaker as in the illustration and drape the thread over the side of the beaker. Observe what happens to the colored water.

Repeat this experiment, but add food coloring to the vial containing salt water and lower it into the beaker of fresh water. Again observe what happens to the colored water.

Based on your observations, which solution is denser—salt water or fresh water? What caused the fluid flows you observed? What do you think would happen if you inserted the vial of colored salt water into the beaker of salt water? What do you think would happen if you eliminated salt water from the experiment and used hot and cold water instead? How would you set up this experiment? Can you think of a way to observe gravity-driven fluid flows without using colored water? What results would you expect if this experiment had been performed in a microgravity environment?

Materials

- 2 large (500-ml) glass beakers or tall drinking glasses
- Large pitcher
- 2 small (5-/10-ml) glass vials
- Thread
- Food coloring
- Salt
- Water
- Spoon or stirring rod

The above experiments should show you that different densities and different temperatures can cause fluid flow. Radically different densities and temperatures were used to magnify the effect of fluid flow. However, very slight density and temperature differences can trigger flow in very still fluids. The next experiment illustrates how an actively growing crystal triggers gravity-driven fluid flows.

Gravity-Driven Fluid Flow During Crystal Growth

In this experiment, you can grow a crystal of a compound called alum and watch the fluid flows it generates by shining a light into the solution.

To begin the experiment, you must create a seed crystal of alum from which your crystal can grow. Do this by dissolving some alum in a small quantity of water in a beaker and then letting the water evaporate over several days. Small crystals should form along the sides and bottom of the beaker. Remove one of the small crystals of alum and attach it to a short length of monofilament fishing line with a dab of silicone cement. Attach several other crystals to other short pieces of line to use as spares if needed.

Prepare the crystal growth solution by dissolving as much powdered or crystalline alum as possible in a beaker of warm water. The amount you will need depends upon the volume and the temperature of the water in the beaker. Refer to the graph in Figure 6-8

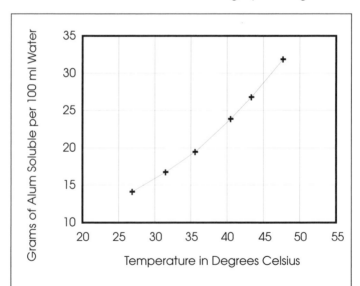

Figure 6-8. This graph will help you estimate how much alum you will need to saturate your water.

Materials

- Alum, or aluminum potassium sulfate $(AlK(SO_4)_2 \cdot 12H_2O^*)$
- Square acrylic box**
- Distilled water
- Stirring rod
- Monofilament fishing line
- Silicone cement
- Beaker
- Slide projector
- Projection screen
- Eye protection
- Hot plate
- Thermometer
- Balance

*Figure 6-8 shows the amount of alum needed for every 100 milliliters (ml) of water you put in the acrylic box.
**Clear acrylic boxes about 10 x 10 x 13 cm in size are available from craft stores. Select a box that has no optical distortions.

to estimate the quantity required. When no more alum can be dissolved in the water, the solution is said to be *saturated*. Pour the solution into a clear acrylic box with a lid. The box will serve as the growth chamber. Let the solution cool to room temperature before proceeding.

Punch a small hole through the center of the lid on the box as shown in Figure 6-9. Thread the seed-crystal line through the hole, letting it drop into the solution until it is several centimeters above the bottom of the box. Secure the line in place with a small amount of tape. Skew the lid so that it rests on the box at a 45-degree angle. This will expose the surface of the solution to the outside air and promote evaporation.

Set the box aside in a place where it can be observed for several days without being disturbed. If the crystal should disappear, remove the lid of the box and let the solution stand for a day or two. Can you guess the reason for doing this? Place a spare seed into the solution and try again.

Record the growth rate of the crystal by measuring its size with a metric ruler. You may want to periodically remove the crystal and weigh it on a balance. Also keep a record of the temperature of the solution. What is the geometric shape of the alum crystal? Does the growth rate of the crystal remain constant? Why or why not? Could a crystal decrease in size? Why?

When the crystal is about the size of a grape, place the vat on a table in front of a projection screen or white wall. Direct the light of a projector through the box so that a shadow of the box is visible on the screen, as shown in Figure 6-9. You should be able to see the outline of the box, the shadow of the crystal, and the line suspending it. After an hour, look for shadowy lines slowly moving about on the screen. Normally, the lines

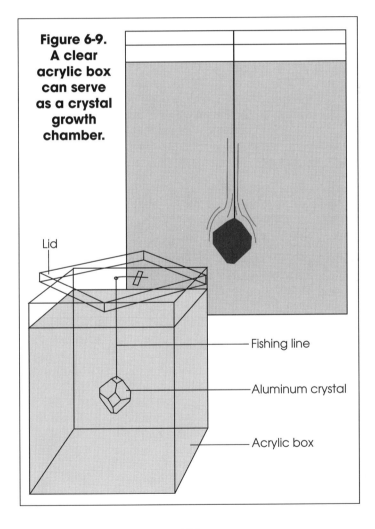

Figure 6-9. A clear acrylic box can serve as a crystal growth chamber.

Lid

Fishing line

Aluminum crystal

Acrylic box

will move upward from the crystal to the surface of the solution. It is important to be very careful while making your observations because any vibration of the solution will affect the formation of these lines.

The lines come from a plume caused by the changing density of the solution around the crystal. As atoms of the dissolved alum are deposited on the crystal surface, the fluid holding them becomes less dense than the liquid farther away from the crystal. Because of its lowered density, the fluid rises up and distorts light passing through the solution. This creates the shadow. Would you expect to see a plume in a crystal vat in microgravity? If you should ever notice a plume going downward, what would that mean? Your crystal size and mass data should provide you with the information you need to answer the question.

Experiment with growing other crystals, such as table salt, sugar, copper sulfate, chrome alum, Rochelle salt, etc. **Caution:** Become familiar with the potential hazards of any of the chemicals you choose and take appropriate safety precautions.

FLAMES IN MICROGRAVITY

Candle flames have something in common with crystal growth solutions. Within a candle flame, wax liquefies and vaporizes, becoming a fluid. This fluid wax flows in response to gravity as crystal growth solutions do.

In microgravity, candle flames are spherical instead of teardrop-shaped. Scientists have gained valuable insights into combustion by conducting flame experiments in drop towers and the space shuttle. In both research environments, a hot wire ignites a flammable material and the combustion process is recorded by movie cameras and other data-collection devices.

You can do your own tests on a candle flame in a microgravity environment in the next project.

A Candle Drop

In this experiment, you can construct a drop chamber that will hold a candle. First, cut a small wood block

**Gravity causes flames to be shaped
like teardrops. In microgravity,
they are spherical.**

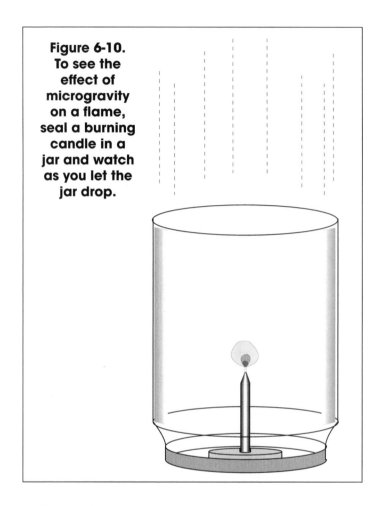

Figure 6-10. To see the effect of microgravity on a flame, seal a burning candle in a jar and watch as you let the jar drop.

to fit inside the lid of a large plastic jar. Attach the block to the inside of the lid with screws coming from the out-side. Place the lid upside down on a flat surface, and in the center of the block, drill a small hole that will hold a birthday candle. Insert a candle into the hole. Fill a cardboard box with empty plastic bags, packing them loosely. Place the box on the floor near the candle. Darken the room. Now light the candle and quickly screw the plastic jar over the candle, as in Figure 6-10.

Observe the shape, brightness, and color of the candle flame. If the candle goes out before you complete your observations, remove the jar and replenish its supply of oxygen by passing it a few times quickly through the air. Relight the candle and seal the jar again. Make sure the lid and jar are screwed together securely before going to the next step.

Lift the jar as high as you can over the box. After making sure the candle is still lit, drop the jar into the box of plastic bags. As the candle drops, observe the shape, brightness, and color of the candle flame. Because the fall is so short, you will probably have to perform several drops to complete your observations. Fluff up the plastic bags before each drop to cushion the impact.

If possible, have an assistant drop the jar so that you can observe the fall from the side. If you have a video camera, try to record the candle's fall. To get a good shot, stand across the room from the candle and zoom in on it before it is dropped. Then have your assistant count down before releasing the jar to prepare you to track the fall with the camera. You will probably have to make several tries to get a good track. When replaying the video, pause on individual frames to study the shape of the candle flame.

Materials

- Clear plastic 2-liter jar and lid—large plastic peanut butter jar
- Wood block
- Screws
- Birthday candles
- Matches
- Drill and bit
- Cardboard box
- Empty plastic bags
- Video camera and monitor (optional)

Did the candle flame change shape during the drop? If so, what new form did the flame take and why? Did the brightness of the candle flame change? If it did change, why? Did the candle flame go out? If it did, when did it go out and why? Were the observations consistent from drop to drop?

A candle flame illustrates very well the complicated physical and chemical processes involved in combustion. Heat from the flame melts the wax at the base of the exposed wick. The liquid wax rises by capillary action up the wick, bringing the wax closer to the hot flame. As a result, the wax vaporizes.

The wax vapors migrate toward the flame surface, breaking down into smaller hydrocarbons en route. At the flame surface, oxygen mixes with the wax vapor at a high temperature. This process radiates heat and light. Oxygen from the surrounding atmosphere migrates toward the flame surface. Taken together, all these processes determine the location of the flame surface and how long it lasts.

Tests of flames on the space shuttle focus on the latter factor, which scientists call flame survivability. Candles onboard the first United States Microgravity Laboratory, launched in June 1992, burned from 45 s to longer than 60 s. Flames in microgravity do not last as long as in gravity because they burn at lower temperatures. The lower temperatures mean the wax does not vaporize as quickly. If the flame temperature and the vaporization rate fall below critical values, the candle flame extinguishes.

The flame temperature is lower in microgravity because oxygen does not travel as rapidly from the surrounding atmosphere to the flame front. In gravity, oxygen gets there by both diffusion and convection. But convection does not exist in microgravity. In convection, gravity pulls the colder, denser parts of a fluid below the hotter, less dense parts. The hot reaction products from the flame rise, and oxygen rushes in toward the flame to replace them. Technically, when there are two different substances involved, the principle that is operating is buoyancy. Because it has the same effect as convection, it is called buoyancy-driven convection.

In this process, solid particles of soot in the region between the flame and the wick rise and burn off, yielding the bright-yellow tip of the flame. The vaporized soot takes a lot of heat with it as it rises; to minimize the loss, the flame narrows toward the top. As a result, the flame looks like a teardrop.

In the absence of buoyancy-driven convection—in microgravity—oxygen gets to the flame only by the much slower process of molecular diffusion. Where there is no "up" or "down," the flame tends toward sphericity. If a lot of heat is lost at the top of the flame, the base of the flame extinguishes and you would see only part of a sphere. The diminished supply of oxygen and fuel causes the flame temperature to lower to the point where little or no soot forms. It also causes the flame to spread far from the wick, reducing the burning rate—the amount of wax consumed per unit time.

7

BIOLOGICAL EFFECTS
OF MICROGRAVITY

One of the most interesting areas of microgravity research focuses on the response of living things to microgravity. The human body, for example, exhibits a number of changes in microgravity.

When a person is on Earth, gravity pulls bodily fluids, such as blood, downward. To prevent blood from pooling in the lower body, muscles in the legs constrict to maintain an even distribution of blood throughout the body. Without the effects of gravity, this muscle constriction drives some of the fluids into the upper body. Thus, in microgravity, there is a tendency for body fluids to shift from the lower to the upper body.

Upper-body fluid pooling is not a serious problem, but it does cause some minor difficulties. Feet tend to get cold because of poor blood circulation there, and the extra fluid around the head causes a feeling of "stuffiness." People also become taller in space because of microgravity. Without the pressure of gravity compressing the spine vertically, the disks between vertebrae expand slightly. This drives vertebrae apart, lengthening the spine. The spine returns to its normal length back on Earth.

An astronaut aboard the space shuttle is being tested for the effects of microgravity on his body.

You can easily investigate these effects with two simple experiments. Fill a round balloon with water, tie it, and hold it by its nozzle. Notice the shape of the balloon. Then, toss the balloon in the air and as it is falling, observe its shape. What does this tell you about upper-body fluid pooling?

You can learn about spine lengthening by accurately measuring your height just before going to bed at night and after you wake in the morning. Instead of standing against a wall to make the measurement, lie flat on the floor with your feet against a wall. Mark the position of the top of your head on the floor. When you make the measurement in the morning, it's important that you do not stand up beforehand. It may sound silly, but you must crawl out of bed to the measuring station, keeping your spine as horizontal as possible. Bed rest simulates some of the effects of microgravity. During the night, your spine lengthens, and it shrinks when you stand up.

Other effects of microgravity on the body are much more important than fluid pooling and spine lengthening. Because it is easy to move about on the space shuttle, leg muscles become very weak in space. Muscles need continual exercise to maintain their tone. For this reason, astronauts exercise daily in space. What kinds of devices do you think they use to exercise? Would a normal treadmill or exercise bicycle work in space? As an interesting project, try to design some exercise devices that can be used in microgravity.

Still another danger in microgravity is the loss of body calcium. This translates to an actual loss of bone mass. The loss is especially worrisome for women astronauts because women suffer in much greater numbers than men from a major calcium deficiency called osteoporosis. A disease of aging, osteoporosis often causes its victims to stoop over time as a result of gradual bone loss from the spine. Calcium loss in microgravity could increase the likelihood of this condition in later life. The reasons for this loss are not well understood and are being actively investigated. Research into astronaut calcium loss may provide clues to preventing osteoporosis in the elderly.

It is difficult to see the effects of microgravity on animals on Earth because the effects arise only after extended periods of microgravity. Furthermore, animal experimentation requires sophisticated tools and analysis techniques, as well as extreme care to avoid undue suffering. Therefore, the topic of animals in microgravity will have to end here. However, there is a lot of fascinating research in this area taking place on the space shuttle. If you are interested in learning more about microgravity research on animals, use your local library resources. Even if your library does not have any resources in this area, librarians can obtain relevant materials through interlibrary loans and electronic information systems.

Research on plants is another matter. You can conduct excellent plant experiments that touch on areas of great interest to microgravity scientists. A prime area is *gravitropism*, the tendency of stems to grow upward and roots to grow downward because of gravity. Gravitropism is also known as *geotropism*; *geo* means Earth. In the next project, you can investigate gravitropism by inverting growing plants.

Gravitropism in Seedlings

Make a seed germination "sandwich" by placing several layers of paper towels and three or four seeds between two sheets of glass. If there are sharp edges on the glass, smooth them with emery cloth. Hold each sandwich together with rubber bands, as shown in Figure 7-1. Make another identical sandwich and stand

Figure 7-1. See the effects of gravity on corn seedlings by growing them between two sheets of glass and then inverting the glass.

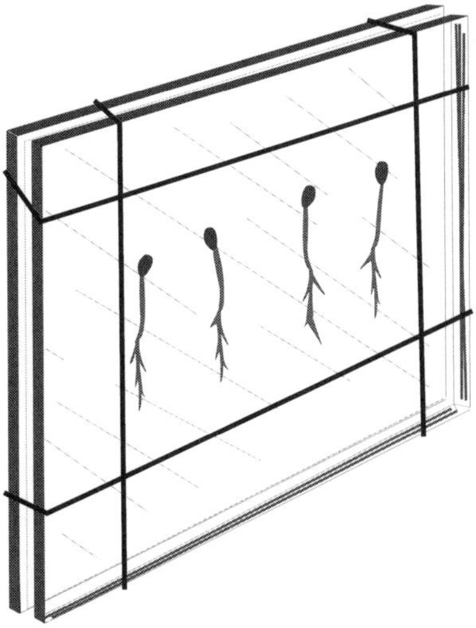

them both upright in a shallow dish of water. Water will soak the paper towels and trigger seed germination. After the developing roots and stems are a few centimeters long, invert one sandwich so that the roots point up and the stems point down. Observe both sandwiches several times each day for a couple of days. Take notes on what you see.

Materials
• Corn seeds
• Four squares of glass, 15 cm x 15 cm
• Emery paper
• Paper towels
• Rubber bands
• Shallow dish

Spinning Plants

Grow bean seedlings in two small flowerpots or paper cups. Tape the pots to the outer edges of an old record turntable, as shown in Figure 7-2. They should be about 30 cm apart and exactly opposite each other across the center of the disk. If you are using a small turntable, you may have to place a larger disk of plywood on it so that you can separate the pots by 30 cm. Place the turntable and plants under a plant grow light and start the turntable spinning at slow speed. Observe the development of the plants for the next two or three days as the spinning continues. What happens? Why?

Gravitropism is just one type of tropism that plants exhibit. *Phototropism* is the tendency of plants to grow toward sunlight. *Hydrotropism* is the tendency of roots to grow toward water. These tropisms are controlled by a group of plant growth hormones called *auxins*. They work by lengthening and shortening plant cells to cause stems and roots to bend in a particular direction.

Microgravity disrupts the process of gravitropism. Without gravity's effects,

Materials
• Old phonograph turntable
• Plant grow light
• 2 small flower pots with bean seedlings
• Masking tape

Figure 7-2. If two bean seedlings are placed on a spinning turntable, do they grow normally?

plants cannot orient themselves to grow in one direction or another. That is not the only reason growing plants in space is difficult. Watering plants is difficult because water does not pour. Even if water is placed directly on the soil, it stays pooled on the surface instead of sinking into the soil.

Using the results of the previous projects, design a plant growth chamber that would work in microgravity. Determine how light, water, and nutrients would be

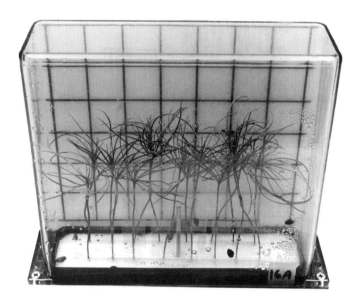

These pine seedlings were grown in Earth orbit to determine the effect of microgravity on their growth.

delivered to the plants. Also determine what kinds of experiments you would perform on the plants. You might even investigate how plants could be grown in space for food for future astronauts. How much planting space would be needed to grow enough food to support one person in space? Could you find some way to recycle spacecraft wastes through your plant system?

8

ABOVE AND
BEYOND

In this chapter, you can become a space traveler of sorts, exploring various corners of the universe. The journey begins with a project that gives a view of the size of the solar system. This and other projects should give you a better idea of Earth as a planet, as well as a closer look at the stars millions of light-years away. Each project can be the starting point for an entire line of research.

PLANETARY EXPLORATION

If you have ever participated in a science fair, you probably know that solar system models are pretty common. They rarely win one of the top prizes, in part because it is difficult to show the proper scale of distances between planets, moons, and the Sun. A model made of Styrofoam balls suspended in a box cannot possibly have the correct scale if it is to fit in a reasonable space. All such a model does is show the order of the planets and their relative size.

To see the scale problem for yourself, choose two spheres of different sizes, such as a basketball and a tennis ball, Styrofoam balls, or even pieces of fruit. The large sphere will represent Earth and the small one will represent the moon. To accurately represent their relative sizes, the large sphere should be about four times larger than the small sphere. The radius of Earth is 6,378 km and the moon's radius is 1,738 km, so the ratio is actually 3.7 to 1.

Take the spheres outside and place them on the ground. Based on the scale of their diameters, separate them a distance you think represents the distance between Earth and the moon. In other words, if the solar system shrank until Earth and moon were the size of the spheres, how far apart would they be?

To check your estimate, first calculate the ratio between the actual Earth-moon distance—384,400 km—and Earth's circumference. You can calculate the circumference using the formula $c = 2\pi r$, where r is Earth's radius. You should get a ratio of 9.59. Wrap a long string around your model of Earth about 9 1/2 times and then stretch that length of string between your models. Earth should be located at one end and the moon at the other. Were your original estimates correct? It might be interesting to ask other people to try estimating this distance to see how well they understand the scale of the solar system.

If you are like most people, you underestimated the distance between Earth and the moon. Your estimates of distances to other planets would probably be even farther off. The table on p. 114 gives the distances and diameters of the planets in our solar system. Notice that many of the planets have different diameters at their equators than they do at the poles. Why do you think this is so? Does this chart provide you enough information to form a hypothesis? If you have formed a hypothesis, is there a way to test it? Also, can you see how the information in the table demonstrates Kepler's third law? See p. 26 in Chapter 2 to refresh your memory.

In the next project, you will use the information in the table to expand your model to the entire solar system.

Solar System Models

To construct an accurate model of the solar system, you must select a scale that is convenient to work with.

For example, if you decided to let the distance between the Sun and Earth be 1 m, the Sun would have to be the size of a small marble and Earth would have to be 100 times smaller than the marble. Mercury would have to be 300 times smaller than the marble! Needless to say, finding spheres that small, much less seeing them, would be difficult.

The real problem with finding a scale you can work with is the Sun. It has a diameter of 1,392,000 km. Everything else in the solar system looks extremely small in comparison. Instead of finding a sphere to represent it, you might use a circular pond in a park as your Sun. The diameter of the pond would set the scale of your model.

For instance, if the pond were 100 m across, what would the scale of the model be? Divide 1,392,000 km by 0.1 km and you would get a scale of 1:13,920,000. To determine how far away Earth should be, divide the distance from Earth to the Sun, 14,500,000 km, by 13,920,000. The distance between your Sun and Earth would have to be 10.74 km!

How far away would Pluto be in the model? According to the table below, Pluto is 39.439 a.u. from the Sun, or 39.44 times farther than Earth. Multiply

PLANET	MEAN DISTANCE TO SUN (A.U.)	EQUATORIAL DIAMETER (KM)	POLAR DIAMETER (KM)	MEAN ORBITAL VELOCITY (KM/S)
Mercury	0.39	4,878	4,878	47.89
Venus	0.72	6,052	6,052	35.04
Earth	1.00	12,756	12,714	29.79
Mars	1.52	6,794	6,760	24.14
Jupiter	5.20	142,984	133,708	13.06
Saturn	9.56	120,536	108,720	9.64
Uranus	19.22	51,118	49,946	6.81
Neptune	30.11	49,528	48,680	5.43
Pluto	39.44	2,280	2,280	4.74

Note: Astronomers use a.u., an abbreviation for astronomical unit, for distances within the solar system. One astronomical unit is the mean distance between Earth and the Sun (149,500,000 km). To convert a.u. to kilometers, multiply by 149,500,000 km.

Materials

• Spheres of different sizes
• Meter stick or metric
tape measure

39.44 times the model distance between the Sun and Earth. Your answer may convince you to find a smaller pond. How big would Earth have to be in your model? Earth's equatorial diameter is 12,756 km. Dividing the diameter by the model scale, you should get an answer of about 0.00092 km, or 92 cm.

Once you have decided on an appropriate scale, lay out all the planets and diameters to the same scale. With the bigger planets, such as Jupiter, you can draw a circle on the ground to represent their sizes.

The next problem in this project is to find some way to bring the model to a science fair. Obviously, the model won't fit into the school building. However, you can present it in still photographs and road maps. Or you can videotape a walking or driving tour of the model.

One thing you will certainly gain from this project is an appreciation of the size of our solar system. Do you now see why the typical science fair solar system model is wrong? This project may also help you understand why human exploration of the solar system is so difficult. How long did it take the Apollo 11 astronauts to get to the moon? How long do you think it would take to get to another planet? What kind of spacecraft would they have to travel in? Where would they get enough food, oxygen, and water for the trip? These are real problems that NASA is studying right now.

PLANET EARTH

To size your solar system model, you calculated the circumference of Earth from its radius. But what if you didn't know the radius? More than 2,100 years ago, no one knew the radius or the circumference of Earth. About that time, Eratosthenes, librarian of Alexandria, Egypt, figured out an ingenious way to accurately estimate the circumference.

How could you determine the circumference of Earth?

His simple, precise method was based on the fact that the bottom of a certain water well in Syene, Egypt, was completely lighted by the Sun at noon on one day of the year. This, he reasoned, meant that the Sun was directly overhead on that day. Eratosthenes also knew that at that same instant far to the north in Alexandria, a stick planted vertically in the ground would cast a shadow, meaning the sunlight must be coming in at an angle to it. Using geometry, Eratosthenes realized that this angle was equal to the angle between the well

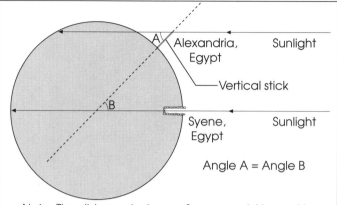

Note: The distance between Syrene and Alexandria has been exaggerated for illustrative purposes.

Figure 8-1. The Greek Eratosthenes calculated the circumference of Earth using this geometry.

and the stick. As shown in Figure 8-1, if the well and the stick were extended toward the center of Earth, they would intersect at an angle *B* equivalent to angle *A*.

Do you recall from geometry why these angles are equal? Note that Eratosthenes had to assume that the Sun's rays were parallel to each other in order to make this deduction. This assumption is correct because Earth is such a great distance from the Sun.

Knowing angle *B* and the distance between Syene and Alexandria, Eratosthenes could calculate the circumference. To measure angle *A*, Eratosthenes used an ancient instrument called a *skaphe*, which is basically a hemispherical bowl with a needle. To determine the distance between the two cities, Eratosthenes hired professional pacers. They were people who could accurately measure a long distance by counting their steps as they walked it.

Angle *A*—and hence angle *B*—turned out to be 7.2 degrees. The distance between the two cities was 5,000 stadia. A *stadia* is an archaic unit of measurement that has been estimated to be approximately 150 to 160 m.

The distance between the two cities is equivalent to an arc on Earth's circumference that is intercepted by the angle *B*. The arc is a fraction of the circumference, which can be thought of as a circle. The fraction is determined by dividing angle *B* by 360 degrees, the number of degrees in a circle. The arc is 7.2/360, or one fiftieth, of a circle. Thus, the total circumference of Earth must be 50 multiplied by 5,000 stadia, or 250,000 stadia.

In the next project, you can repeat Eratosthenes's measurement.

Measuring Earth's Circumference

For this project, you will need the help of someone who lives a few hundred kilometers north or south of you. Fortunately, this variation of Eratosthenes's measurement does not require that one site be directly under the Sun at noon. If each person takes a measurement of the angle of the Sun at noon on the same day, the measurements can be combined to determine Earth's circumference. As shown in Figure 8-2, you can

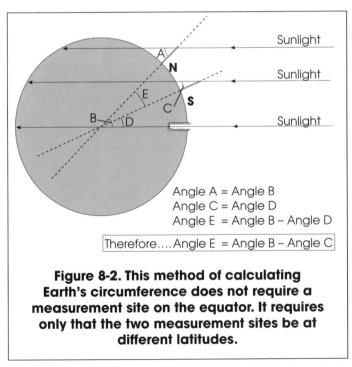

Angle A = Angle B
Angle C = Angle D
Angle E = Angle B – Angle D

Therefore.... Angle E = Angle B – Angle C

Figure 8-2. This method of calculating Earth's circumference does not require a measurement site on the equator. It requires only that the two measurement sites be at different latitudes.

determine the angle between the two sites by subtracting the smaller angle from the larger one.

The two sites do not have to be directly north or south of each other as long as the measurements are made at local noon—when the Sun is at its highest point in the sky at each location. Can you guess why? You must know the north-south distance between the two sites, however. You can get it from a road map by figuring the vertical distance between the latitude lines at the two sites. Or, if the sites lie along a north-south direction, you may be able to use a car odometer to measure the distance.

To make this method work, you will need good communications with your research partner. You might try contacting the person with a computer through the Internet "information highway." That way, it will be easy to work out procedures and share data.

After you have found a research partner, select a day for the measurement. Both sites must have clear skies on the same day. Each of you will need an angle-measuring device. To make one, attach a protractor to a stick using a straight pin, as shown in Figure 8-3. Also attach a string to the pin, and tie a washer or nut to the other end. This will serve as a plumb line to help you set up the stick vertically. Getting the stick perfectly vertical is extremely important. An error of a single degree in aligning the stick can throw off your final answer by hundreds of kilometers.

Materials

- Protractor
- Straight pin
- Stick
- String
- Heavy washer, nut, or other small weight
- Road map
- Magnetic compass

The next important step is to determine true north at each location. You can use a magnetic compass if you make a correction for the difference between magnetic north and true north. This correction is a small angle called the *declination*. You can find the declination for your location on a topographic map of the

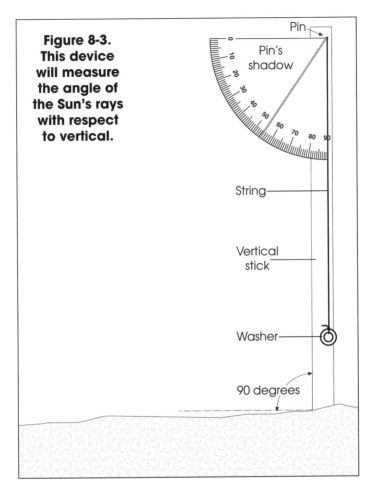

Figure 8-3. This device will measure the angle of the Sun's rays with respect to vertical.

Pin

Pin's shadow

0
10
20
30
40
50
60
70
80
90

String

Vertical stick

Washer

90 degrees

region. Get a map from the reference section of a library or from a camping supply store and follow the instructions for adding or subtracting the degrees of declination from magnetic north.

Mark the direction of true north by drawing a line on the ground at each measurement site. On the selected day, each person should insert the stick into the ground, adjusting it until it is perfectly vertical. The measurement of the Sun's angle must take place when it is noon at each site. Do not use your watch to determine when local noon is! Why? Local noon is the moment when the Sun is highest in the sky for that day. The shadow of the stick points toward true north at local noon. Align the protractor along your true north line, with the zero-degree line pointing north. When it is local noon, take the measurement of the Sun's angle by noting where the pin's shadow falls on the protractor.

When you have the angle from each site, subtract the smaller measurement from the larger one. This is the angle between your two sticks. Divide 360 degrees by the angle and multiply the answer by the north-south distance between your two locations. The result is your measurement for Earth's circumference. How close does it come to 40,074 km?

METEORITE CRATERS

Asteroids and comets flying through space some-times get caught in Earth's gravity and fall into the atmosphere. If they survive the intense heating caused by friction with air molecules, they hit Earth's surface and make craters. Once they hit Earth, they are called *meteorites*. These meteorites have been striking Earth since our planet was created over four and a half billion years ago. Most of the craters are no longer visible because of erosion. However, if you aim a small tele-scope at Earth's companion, the moon, you can see thousands of craters. Craters formed billions of years ago are still visible because the erosion rate on the moon is far less than that on Earth.

In recent years, interest has grown in how meteorite impacts have affected Earth's climate and life. Large asteroids or comets can devastate large areas. Scien-tists have speculated that they can throw up huge amounts of earth that block sunlight over large areas, causing temperatures to drop. Such an artificial winter, many scientists believe, may have led to the extinction of the dinosaurs 65 million years ago. A huge buried crater discovered in recent decades on the northern edge of the Yucatán Peninsula in Mexico has been dated to that time period. The crater is 200 to 300 km in diameter and was produced by an object 6 to 10 km in diameter.

In the next project, you can explore the relationship between meteorites and the craters they produce. Dry sand will serve as Earth's surface, and ball bearings and marbles will be the meteorites.

Making Craters

Fill a shallow cardboard box with sand and smooth over its surface. Standing carefully near the top of a tall stepladder or leaning *slightly* out a second-story window, drop a ball bearing into the box of sand on the ground below. The impact should produce a crater as shown in Figure 8-4. After carefully removing the ball bearing, measure the diameter and depth of the crater with a millimeter ruler. Record these measurements in a data table that includes the mass of the ball bearing and the distance you dropped it. Make a sketch of the crater as it would appear from the side.

Repeat the test using a marble the size of the ball bearing. Be sure to drop it from the same height. Again, measure and sketch the crater produced. Is there any

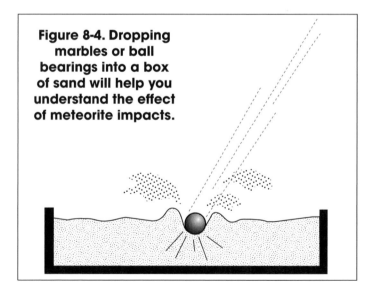

Figure 8-4. Dropping marbles or ball bearings into a box of sand will help you understand the effect of meteorite impacts.

Materials

- Shallow cardboard or wooden box
- Enough fine, dry sand to fill the box
- Marbles of different sizes
- Ball bearings of different sizes
- Meter stick or metric tape measure
- Metric beam balance
- Small metric ruler with millimeter divisions
- Eye protection
- Tall stepladder or second-floor window
- Data table and pencil

relationship between the size of the crater and the mass of the object? How fast were the objects traveling when they struck the sand? Refer to the altitude tracking project on p. 53 for help. Can you determine the force of the impact? Newton's second law of motion, on p. 40, will come in handy here.

Next, experiment with changing the velocity of the impactor. Stand next to the box and throw the ball bearing into the sand as fast as you can. **Caution:** When you do this, make sure no one is nearby and wear eye protection in case the impact throws sand back into your face. How does the velocity of the impact affect the size and shape of the crater?

Finally, drop marbles or ball bearings of different sizes from the same height so that you can compare the diameter of the impactor with the crater size. Use either marbles or ball bearings, but not both, to make the comparison. Why is this important?

After you have completed your studies of craters and impactors, look at the surface of the moon through a telescope or in pictures. What do the shapes and sizes of the craters tell you about the objects that struck there? Why do many craters overlap? What does that tell you about the relative ages of the craters? Also examine pictures of Mercury, Mars, and the moons of other planets. Are there differences in the craters found on different worlds? Research the 1994 comet Levy/Shoemaker 9 impact on Jupiter. It produced no craters, but scientists made many discoveries as a result of it. What were they?

EXPLORING THE STARS

Far beyond our solar system are the stars. The stars are so far away, it's amazing we know anything at all about them. But scientists have ways of discovering what they're made of, their size, and how they move.

One of the easiest ways to begin learning about stars, as well as the motion of your own planet, is to photograph star trails. Stars do not actually leave trails in the sky; star trails show up only on camera film after a long exposure. If you mount a camera on a tripod and leave the shutter open for several minutes, the image of the stars stretches out into lines because of Earth's rotation. The stars appear to move slowly across the sky, just as the Sun does.

If you take long exposures of stars above the equator, you will see that their path is similar to the one the Sun takes—up from the horizon in the East and down to the West. But trails of stars above the North Pole are concentric circles with the North Star at the center. Can you guess why? Remember that the North Star is directly over the North Pole, which does not move with Earth's rotation.

The lengths of the star trails depend upon how long the exposure is—how long you leave the shutter open. The next project shows you how to go about taking your own photographs of star trails.

Star Trail Photography

To take star trail pictures, go out on a very dark and clear night to an open area with few house or street lights. The moon should be no more than about one quarter full; moonlight lights up the sky, making it difficult to see faint stars. Set up the tripod in a level location and mount the camera to it. Aim the camera at some stars and adjust the camera controls to the B setting. On this setting, the shutter stays open as long as you hold down the button. To avoid jiggling the camera as the picture is taken, hold the shutter open

Materials

- Camera with manual control options
- Cable release
- Stable tripod
- Color slide or print film

with a cable release. The cable release allows you to control the shutter from a distance.

Now, remove the lens cap and time the exposure as you take a picture. Try different exposure lengths for the same region of the sky. Later, when you develop the pictures, you will learn which exposures work best for the kind of film you are using.

If you take very long exposures (several hours or more) you will have to adjust the aperture of the camera to reduce the amount of light reaching the film. Otherwise, the sky background will become too bright on the film and will blend in with the star trails. While you are taking the pictures, you may get lucky and capture the trail of a satellite on the film. You can distinguish it from the star trails because its trail intersects them, rather than running parallel to them. You may also catch the streak of some bright meteors in your photos.

Here is an important reminder if your camera has an electronic shutter control, as many new adjustable cameras do. As you hold the shutter open, power drains from the battery. Be sure to bring spare batteries along if you are planning an all-night photography session.

Did you notice that the trails are different colors? The colors have to do with the nature of the stars. What do the colors tell us?

STAR COLORS

Astronomers can deduce much about a star from the color of the light it gives off. They can determine its temperature, its chemical composition, its size, and even its motion toward or away from Earth by looking at the spectrum of wavelengths in the light. The instruments with which astronomers analyze starlight are called *spectroscopes.*

Star trails around the North Star are concentric circles.

Starlight originates from the atoms of gas that make up the *photosphere*, or surface, of a star. These atoms collide with each other millions of times every second. The higher the temperature, the greater the rate of collisions. The atoms absorb and release energy in these collisions in packets of light called *photons*. The higher the energy released during a collision, the shorter the wavelength of light emitted from it. The wavelength of the light determines its color.

Photons are also released in the filament of an electric light bulb. As the temperature of the filament rises, it begins radiating reddish light. When the filament becomes much hotter, it radiates bluish light. Thus, the color it radiates is an indicator of the filament's temperature. Similarly, stars that radiate a great amount of red light are much cooler than stars that radiate a great amount of blue light. Every star radiates a spectrum of different colors of varying intensities. A spectroscope aimed at a star reveals this spectrum by separating the colors and displaying them in a band, lined up in the same sequence as the colors in a rainbow. These stellar spectra serve as star thermometers.

A star's spectrum can also identify the chemical elements in the photosphere. Each element radiates light in a unique combination of colors, or wavelengths, that is as distinctive as a fingerprint. Since astronomers know the "spectral signature" of each element, they can identify the elements in distant stars by directing a spectroscope at them. And since the movement of the stars with respect to Earth causes a slight shift in wavelength, spectroscopes can also detect their motion.

By classifying stars into spectral categories, astronomers can estimate their age, reconstruct their histories, and speculate on what they may be like in the future. Astronomers prefer stellar spectra collected by orbiting spacecraft rather than spectra collected by Earth-based telescopes because the atmosphere filters some of the light. Spacecraft can see not only all colors of visible light, but also invisible forms of light, or electromagnetic energy, including infrared, ultraviolet, X-ray, and gamma ray wavelengths. These wavelengths are filtered out by the atmosphere, so they do not reach ground-based spectroscopes.

In the next project, you can build your own spectroscope and analyze the light sources around you.

Analytical Spectroscope

To make your spectroscope, use the patterns in Figures 8-5 and 8-6 for the spectroscope housing. Take them to a copy machine and enlarge them about 200 percent. Make two enlarged copies of Figure 8-5, and be sure to include the black measurement grid and eyepiece square when you enlarge Figure 8-6.

Cut out the enlarged patterns from Figure 8-5. Place them on heavy posterboard that is dark on at least one side, and tape them in the arrangement shown in Figure 8-6. Then cut the resulting pattern from the posterboard and lightly score the fold lines with a razor-blade knife. If you mistakenly cut all the way through a fold line, just tape the pieces back together. Fold the housing to look like a pie-shaped box and tape the open edges together. Make sure the inside surface is dark.

Cut out the enlarged front panel and eyepiece square from Figure 8-6, trace them onto posterboard, and then cut them out. To cut out the rectangles on the interior of the pieces, first tape the paper patterns to the posterboard pieces. Then, on a cutting surface, cut the holes using a razor-blade knife against a straightedge.

The eyepiece square will fit into the small opening in the spectroscope housing, but first you must attach an eyepiece to the side of the square that will go inside the spectroscope. The eyepiece is a holographic diffraction grating, a piece of plastic film through which you will view the spectrum of a light source. Cut a piece of diffraction grating large enough to cover the hole in the eyepiece square. You must handle the grating by the edges because skin oils can damage it.

To orient the grating correctly, look through it at a fluorescent light. Turn the grating so that the rainbow colors you see appear in vertical bars to the right and left of the light. Tape the grating in this orientation behind the hole in the eyepiece square. Then tape the eyepiece square to the spectroscope housing so that the grating is on the inside. With the grating in the correct orientation,

Materials
• Heavy posterboard (must be dark on one side)
• Aluminum foil
• Pencil
• Cellophane tape
• Black tape
• Scissors
• Razor-blade knife
• Straightedge
• Holographic diffraction grating*

* available from:
–Arbor Scientific, P.O. Box 2750, Ann Arbor, MI 48106-2750, Phone: 1-800-367-6695
–Flinn Scientific, P.O. Box 219, 131 Flinn Street, Batavia, IL 60510, Phone: 1-800-452-1261
–Learning Technologies, Inc., 59 Walden Street, Cambridge, MA 02140, Phone: 1-800-537-8703

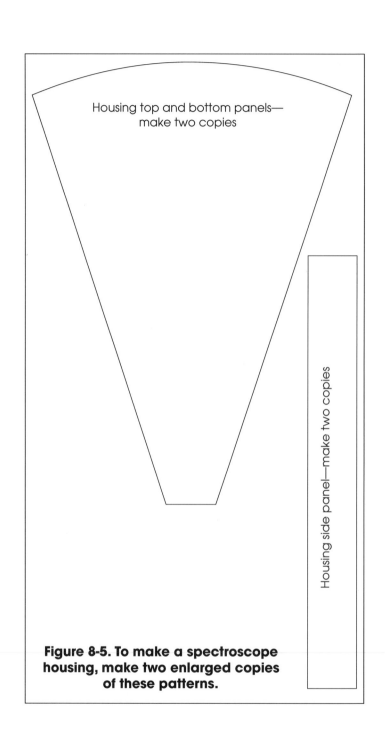

Housing top and bottom panels—
make two copies

Housing side panel—make two copies

**Figure 8-5. To make a spectroscope
housing, make two enlarged copies
of these patterns.**

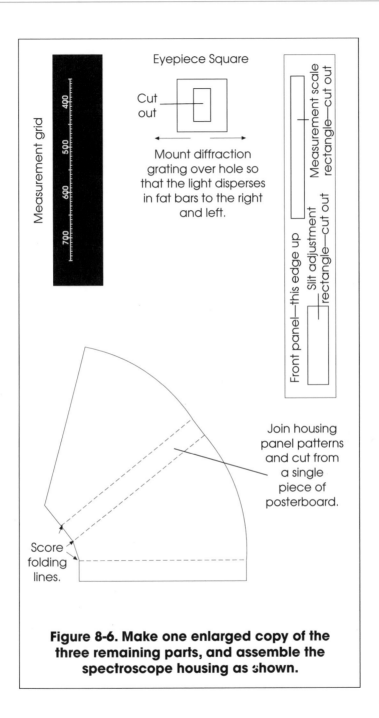

Measurement grid

Eyepiece Square

Cut out

Mount diffraction grating over hole so that the light disperses in fat bars to the right and left.

Measurement scale rectangle—cut out

Front panel—this edge up

Slit adjustment rectangle—cut out

Join housing panel patterns and cut from a single piece of posterboard.

Score folding lines.

Figure 8-6. Make one enlarged copy of the three remaining parts, and assemble the spectroscope housing as shown.

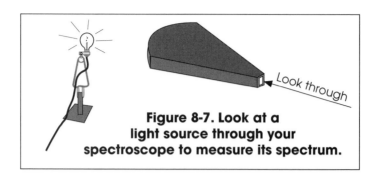

Figure 8-7. Look at a light source through your spectroscope to measure its spectrum.

note which side of the housing is the top and which is the bottom.

Cut out the enlarged black measurement grid from the copier paper (not the posterboard). Tape this paper grid over the long slit on the front panel piece. First, orient the front panel as it will be in the housing as viewed through the eyepiece—with the slit in the upper right-hand corner. Carefully align the grid with the hole so that when you hold the front panel piece to the light, the grid is illuminated by light passing through the paper. Trim any excess tape.

Tape the front panel to the wide opening in the spectroscope housing, with the scale on the inside upper right-hand corner. Make sure the seams are closed so that no light escapes through them. The final step in making the spectroscope is to close off the second opening on the front panel, leaving a small vertical slit about 1 mm wide. Using a razor-blade knife, make the slit in a piece of aluminum foil laid out on a cutting surface. Try to make the cut as smooth as possible because any roughness will show up in the spectrum as dark streaks perpendicular to the slot. With the slit oriented vertically in the center of the open rectangle on the front panel, temporarily tape the foil in place.

Now that you have constructed the spectroscope, you must calibrate it to a known light source. Use a standard fluorescent light, not a broad-spectrum fluorescent light. Aim the spectroscope at the light, as shown in Figure 8-7. Look through the eyepiece and point the slit toward the light. You should notice a broad band of rainbow colors underneath the measurement scale. Find the bright-green line within the band. Shift the foil to the right or left until the bright-green line in the display is located at 546 nanometers on the scale. Retape the slit in place. Your spectroscope is now calibrated.

Investigate different light sources with your spectroscope. Compare incandescent light, fluorescent light, and sunlight with one another. You can point the spectroscope directly at the Sun without fear of harming your eyes, but make sure you don't accidentally look at the Sun without the spectroscope. Also examine neon signs and streetlights. Many high school physics departments have spectrum tubes, which produce light from different gases. Ask a physics teacher for permission to set up the apparatus so that you can study the spectra from these gases.

What do you observe about the spectra from the different light sources? Do you think there is any relationship between the color, brightness, and temperature of a light? Use a dimmer switch on a clear light bulb to find out. Compare the solar spectrum at midday and at sunset. Are there any differences? What do spectra tell us about the nature of stars and other objects in space? Compare your observations of spectra of different lights to the colors seen in the star trails project.

Some light sources give off a *continuous spectrum*, which is a continuous band of colors ranging from red to violet as you see in rainbows. A band of color interrupted by dark lines is called an *absorption spectrum*. That occurs when the light from a star, for example, passes through a cloud of gas such as hydrogen before reaching the spectroscope. As a result, some wavelengths of light are absorbed by the hydrogen atoms and appear as dark lines on the spectrum. Such a situation occurs when a star is located inside or behind a gas cloud or *nebula*. If the gas is of a certain composition, it will reradiate the light at different wavelengths, producing an *emission spectrum*. This kind of spectrum looks like bright lines on a black background. The light from fluorescent tubes and neon lights produces emission spectra.

SPACE PHOTOGRAPHY

One of the greatest benefits from the space program is the millions of photographs of Earth taken from space. Some pictures are taken by astronauts as they orbit Earth, and many others are taken by weather satellites and satellites that study Earth's surface. Scientists make extensive use of these pictures to forecast weather and to study the processes that shape Earth. Pictures from space are also used for prospecting, studying crops, assessing the health of rain forests, and protecting our environment.

There are many fascinating projects you can do that revolve around space photography. You might compare satellite photographs of the city you live in with city street maps to learn about trends in city growth and sources of pollution. You could examine photographs of wilderness areas to study the impact of logging, mining, and recreation on animal habitats. Or you could track where pollution enters rivers over time to see how environmental protection measures are working.

In many of these projects, you may need to have computers interpret the space photographs. Computer interpretation is done as a matter of routine at most colleges and universities, and they may be willing to provide you with data. If you live in a city with a university or college, call the departments of biology, geography, geology, and meteorology to find out if anyone is doing space photography research. Researchers are usually happy to advise students and sometimes give them access to their facilities.

Other sources of space photography include your local branch of the U.S. Weather Service. Meteorologists may be willing to provide you with satellite weather pictures they no longer need. Television news services may also be able to provide you with images.

Deforestation

Regrowth

Isolated Forest

Forest

This composite photograph of the Brazilian rain forest was made with data from two orbiting satellites.

Pictures of Earth's land surface can be obtained from the following addresses. Write them for details:

Earth Data Analysis Center
University of New Mexico
Albuquerque, NM 87131-6031

Earth Observation Satellite Company (EOSAT)
4300 Forbes Blvd.
Lanham, MD 20706

Media Services Branch
Still Photography Library
NASA Lyndon B. Johnson Space Center
P.O. Box 58425, Mail Code AP3
Houston, TX 77258

U.S. Geological Survey
EROS Data Center
Earth Science Information Center
Sioux Falls, SD 57198

As a final source of Earth photography, try download-ing images from the Internet. Refer to the resources section for possible sources.

EXPERIMENTING IN SPACE

By now, you should have a desire to do some actual experiments in space. You might think you have to wait until you are a scientist to fly experiments in space, but you can do it right now through a special program offered by NASA. It is called the Self-Con-tained Payload Program—popularly known as the Get Away Special (GAS).

This program allows anyone who wants to conduct an experiment in microgravity to use the extra space available on many shuttle missions in the cavernous payload bay. The experiments are carried in canisters that attach to the walls of the payload bay or a bridge running across it. Anyone with a scientific or techno-logic experiment can rent a canister from NASA. That includes individuals, industry, and schools.

The cost of the canister, including its launch into space and return, ranges between $8,000 and $27,000 for most users, but NASA offers special rates to educa-tional institutions. These rates are $3,000 for the smallest canister, which is 0.07 cubic meters (cu m) and is capa-ble of carrying 27.4 kg; $5,000 for a canister of the

Technicians walk across the bridge in the payload bay of the space shuttle *Discovery*. The canisters underneath the bridge carry experiments that must be conducted in microgravity.

same dimensions that can carry 45.4 kg; and $10,000 for a large canister of 0.14 cu m, capable of carrying 90.7 kg.

You may think that these costs are way out of line for your means, but you don't have to pay them yourself. Many local businesses, industry, and civic organizations would be delighted to invest in future scientists if presented with a good research proposal.

The first step in beginning a GAS project is to form a research team at your school with teacher advisers. As an officially sponsored school project, your research will qualify for the lower rental fees. Meet with your team to discuss ideas for experiments and to develop the proposal you will write to raise funds from organizations.

You also will need to find out NASA's requirements for GAS projects. For example, one of the requirements is that the experiments be self-contained; if the experiment requires electricity, batteries must be part of the experiment package. Another is that it must be able to be run with minimal human intervention; for each experiment, the crew members will flip as many as six switches during the flight, to, say, turn the experiment on or off or control it in some other way. To get all the rules, write to the address below.

Shuttle Small Payloads Program Customer
    Support Manager
Code 745
NASA Goddard Space Flight Center
Greenbelt, MD 20771

CONTINUE THE ADVENTURE

The projects in this book can be the beginning of many adventures. Only your imagination and desire limit how far you carry these projects. If you work hard and follow your dreams, you can do just about anything—even fly into outer space. So what's keeping you from starting?

RESOURCES

SPACELINK

NASA Spacelink is a computer information service that allows individuals to receive news about current NASA programs, activities, and other space-related information including historical material, space images of the planets, astronaut data, and even entire publications. Anyone with a computer and modem can access NASA Spacelink. The access telephone number is 205-895-0028. The data word format is 8 bits, no parity, and 1 stop bit. Spacelink is also accessible through the Internet system at the following addresses:

Telnet: spacelink.msfc.nasa.gov
World Wide Web: http://spacelink.msfc.nasa.gov
Gopher: spacelink.msfc.nasa.gov
Anonymous FTP: spacelink.msfc.nasa.gov
Internet TCP/IP: 192.149.89.61

THE INTERNET

Spacelink is just one of many space-related electronic information services available through the Internet system. You may be able to get access to the Internet through a computer and modem at your school. Unlike Spacelink, which anyone can contact just by calling, you need to access the Internet through system servers. Many servers are located at universities that permit local schools to use them. Check with your teachers at school to determine if they have access to the Internet. If not, encourage them to gain access. Because new services are added daily to the Internet, it is not possible to provide an up-to-date list here. Internet directories are available at bookstores and libraries. A little exploring on the Internet will channel you into an amazing variety of data sources that will put you right into the middle of space science research.

AMATEUR RADIO

If you have ever had an urge to talk with space shuttle astronauts while they are in space, you may be able to do so with amateur radio. The American Radio Relay League conducts radio experiments with the space shuttle on many flights. This program is called SAREX, or Shuttle Amateur Radio Experiment. Through the experiment, amateur radio operators, known as "ham radio operators," attempt to contact radio-licensed astronauts in space through a special radio receiver and transmitter installed on the shuttle. As a part of each experiment, students at select schools are given an opportunity to make contact as well. To find out more about this opportunity and about space science–related radio science projects, write:

American Radio Relay League
225 Main Street
Newington, CT 06111
Phone: 1-800-326-9426

NASA CENTERS

Additional information about space science research and NASA programs can be obtained by writing to NASA directly. NASA has divided the country into service regions. Write the NASA center that serves the state you live in.

For Alaska, Arizona, California, Hawaii, Idaho, Montana, Nevada, Oregon, Utah, Washington, and Wyoming, write:

NASA Ames Research Center
Moffett Field, CA 94035

For Connecticut, Delaware, the District of Columbia, Maine, Maryland, Massachusetts, New Hampshire, New Jersey, New York, Pennsylvania, Rhode Island, and Vermont, write:

NASA Goddard Space Flight Center
Greenbelt, MD 20771

For Colorado, Kansas, Nebraska, New Mexico, North Dakota, Oklahoma, South Dakota, and Texas, write:

NASA Johnson Space Center
Houston, TX 77058

For Florida, Georgia, Puerto Rico, and the Virgin Islands, write:

NASA Kennedy Space Center
Kennedy Space Center, FL 32899

For Kentucky, North Carolina, South Carolina, Virginia, and West Virginia, write:

NASA Langley Research Center
Hampton, VA 23681-0001

For Illinois, Indiana, Michigan, Minnesota, Ohio, and Wisconsin, write:

NASA Lewis Research Center
21000 Brookpark Road
Cleveland, OH 44135

For Alabama, Arkansas, Iowa, Louisiana, Missouri, and Tennessee, write:

NASA Marshall Space Flight Center
Huntsville, AL 35812

For Mississippi, write:

NASA John C. Stennis Space Center
Stennis Space Center, MS 39529

For information specifically related to planetary exploration, write:

Jet Propulsion Laboratory
4800 Oak Grove Drive
Pasadena, CA 91109

For California cities near the Dryden Flight Research Facility, write:

NASA Dryden Flight Research Facility
Edwards, CA 93523

For Virginia and Maryland's Eastern Shores, write:

Wallops Flight Facility
Wallops Island, VA 2337

Other sources of information regarding space science research include local science and technology museums and astronomical observatories.

FOR FURTHER READING

Additional information about space science research and projects can be obtained from the following references:

Apfel, Necia. *Astronomy Projects for Young Scientists*. New York: Arco Publications, 1984.
Baker, D. *Experiments in Space*. Vero Beach, Fla.: Rourke Enterprises, 1986.
Gardner, R. *Projects in Space Science*. New York: Julian Messner, 1988.
Gardner, R. *Robert Gardner's Challenging Science Experiments*. New York: Franklin Watts, 1993.
McKay, D., and B. Smith. *Space Science Projects for Young Scientists*. New York: Franklin Watts, 1986.
Millspaugh, B. *Aviation and Space Science Projects*. Blue Ridge Summit, Pa.: TAB Books, 1992.
Moulton, R. *First to Fly*. Minneapolis: Lerner Publications Co., 1983.
Vogt, G. *The Space Shuttle: Projects for Young Scientists*. New York: Franklin Watts, 1983.

INDEX